||| || ||| ||||| ||||| |||| |||||||||||||||| ||| |||

✔ **KT-230-753**

Psychology and Crime

NOT TO BE TAKEN AWAY

What does a criminological psychologist do? The popular image is that of a modern-day Sherlock Holmes helping the police to solve crimes and mysteries, but the reality is much more complex. *Psychology and Crime* is a new introduction to the topic of criminological psychology that helps dispel these popular myths by providing a comprehensive overview of the topic of criminological psychology.

The book includes both classic and contemporary psychological theory and research on a range of criminological issues including the nature, measurement and causes of crime, police work and offender profiling, eyewitness memory, trial procedures, jury decision making and the treatment of crime. Putwain and Sammons have produced an introductory text which covers the material on this topic in the A2 components of the AQA-B, OCR and Edexcel A-Level specifications. *Psychology and Crime* is also ideal for undergraduate students looking for an introduction to criminological psychology and for students studying psychology and media. It will also be useful for those who work in fields related to criminology such as the police and probation services,

Psychology and crime

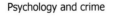

David P   Foundation and

a regular   **mons** is Head

of Psych   They are both

experien

1001214   364.3 PUT

The Henley College

THE HENLEY COLLEGE LIBRARY

Routledge Modular Psychology

Series editors: Cara Flanagan is a freelance academic author and an experienced teacher and examiner for AS and A2 level psychology. Philip Banyard is Associate Senior Lecturer in Psychology at Nottingham Trent University and has 20 years experience as a Chief Examiner for AS and A2 level Psychology.

The *Routledge Modular Psychology* series is a completely new approach to introductory level psychology, tailor-made to the new modular style of teaching. Each short book covers a topic in more detail than any large textbook can, allowing teacher and student to select material exactly to suit any particular course or project.

The books have been written especially for those students new to higher level study, whether at school, college or university. They include specially designed features to help with technique, such as a model essay at an average level with an examiner's comments to show how extra marks can be gained. The authors are all examiners and teachers at the introductory level.

The *Routledge Modular Psychology* texts are all user friendly and accessible and use the following features:

- practice essays with specialist commentary to show how to achieve a higher grade
- chapter summaries to assist with revision
- progress and review exercises
- glossary of key terms
- summaries of key research
- further reading to stimulate ongoing study and research
- cross-referencing to other books in the series

For more details on our AS, A2 and *Routledge Modular Psychology* publications visit our website at www.a-levelpsychology.co.uk

Also available in this series (titles listed by syllabus section):

Psychology and Crime

*David Putwain
and Aidan Sammons*

Routledge
Taylor & Francis Group

LONDON AND NEW YORK

First published 2002 by Routledge
27 Church Road, Hove, East Sussex BN3 2FA

Simultaneously published in the USA and Canada
by Routledge
270 Madison Avenue, New York NY 10016

Reprinted 2002, 2003 and 2008

Routledge is an imprint of the Taylor & Francis Group, an Informa business

© 2002 Psychology Press

Typeset in Times and Frutiger by Keystroke,
Jacaranda Lodge, Wolverhampton
Printed and bound in Great Britain
by TJ International, Padstow, Cornwall

This publication has been produced with paper manufactured to strict
environmental standards and with pulp derived from sustainable forests.

Cover design by Terry Foley

All rights reserved. No part of this book may be reprinted or
reproduced or utilised in any form or by any electronic, mechanical,
or other means, now known or hereafter invented, including
photocopying and recording, or in any information storage or
retrieval system, without permission in writing from the publishers.

British Library Cataloguing in Publication Data
A catalogue record for this book is available from the British Library

Library of Congress Cataloging in Publication Data
Putwain, David.
Psychology and crime / David Putwain and Aidan Sammons.
p. cm. – (Routledge modular psychology)
Includes bibliographical references and index.
ISBN 0–415–25299–7 – ISBN 0–415–25300–4 (pbk.)
1. Criminal psychology. 2. Crime–Psychological aspects. 3. Criminal justice,
Administration of–Psychological aspects. 4. Criminology.
I. Sammons, Aidan. II. Title. III. Series
HV6080 .P87 2002
364.3–dc21   2001058923

ISBN 978–0–415–25300–0 (Pbk)

Contents

Figures and tables

Figures

Tables

Acknowledgements

The authors gratefully acknowledge the assistance of Phillip Banyard for providing examiner's comments to the OCR specimen question and Donald Pennington for examiner's comments to the AQA-B specimen question. We would also like to thank Nicola Simpson for reading draft chapters and making helpful comments, Cara Flanagan for invaluable editorial assistance and the reviewers for their insightful criticisms.

1

Introduction

◼ What is criminological psychology?

The aim of this book is to provide a general introduction to a range of psychological research into crime. It is chiefly aimed at students studying the various A2-Level courses which include criminological psychology as an option topic, but, it is hoped, will be useful to any reader requiring basic information on criminological psychology. The authors have attempted to cover all of the topics in which students will be interested. This chapter introduces the subject and describes some of the ways in which psychology can be used to understand crime. Chapter 2 examines a range of different approaches to defining and measuring crime. Chapters 3 and 4 discuss a number of different psychological explanations for offending, including biological, personality and social theories of crime. Chapter 5 examines the police and looks at a range of issues such as police bias and interviewing techniques, whilst Chapter 6 examines a more direct application of psychology to policing in the form of offender profiling. The focus of Chapters 7 and 8 is the courtroom and a range of research is discussed concerning witness testimony, trial procedures and jury processes. Chapter 9 examines the ways in which the judicial system responds to crime and looks also at the effectiveness of psychological treatments for crime and crime prevention programmes. Finally, Chapter

10, which is aimed specifically at A2-Level students, gives guidance on answering exam questions and includes comments from senior A2-Level examiners.

WHAT IS CRIMINOLOGICAL PSYCHOLOGY?

Imagine asking a member of the general public the following questions:

- What is a criminological psychologist?
- What does a criminological psychologist do?
- What type of clients do criminological psychologists work with?

The answers to these questions are likely to be informed by high-profile media cases and successful films and TV programmes. This leads to a distorted view of the criminological psychologist as some kind of modern-day Sherlock Holmes, helping the police solve crimes and mysteries. In reality, psychologists working with the police do much more than help solve crimes. Psychologists are involved in rehabilitating offenders, providing expert advice in court cases, assessing both offenders and victims, preventing crime and much more.

Psychological methods have been used by the police and legal system since the early 1900s but it was not until the 1960s that **criminological psychology** as a specific branch of psychology emerged. It is just one of a number of disciplines devoted to policing and legal practices which include criminology, sociology, psychiatry and law.

The contribution that psychology can make to criminological issues tends to reflect the strengths and weaknesses of psychology as a discipline. On the positive side, psychologists undergo rigorous training in research methodology, and are therefore well placed to carry out their own investigations and experiments and to comment on and evaluate the work of others. On the negative side, psychology tends to emphasise *individual* factors at the expense of *social* factors. For example, psychological explanations of criminal behaviour tend to concentrate on why *individuals* become offenders by considering factors such as personality and brain function. In contrast, sociological approaches tend to emphasise *social* factors such as poverty and social class. Consequently, psychological approaches tend to underestimate the amount of crime and sociological approaches tend to overestimate the amount of crime (Harrower 1988). Neither approach is foolproof and each complements the other. When taken in isolation, each approach can only provide part of the whole picture, but when taken together they provide a more comprehensive understanding of crime.

Applying psychological principles to crime

Criminological psychology, along with clinical and organisational psychology, is an example of applied rather than 'pure' psychology. Pure psychology usually refers to the type of research carried out by academics in universities (although this is not always the case). Academic psychologists may be investigating topics with direct relevance to the real world (e.g. can children provide reliable eyewitness accounts?) but the majority of this type of research is carried out in the laboratory. This has the advantage of controlling for the kinds of confounding variables encountered in real-life research. However, a drawback of this approach is that the external validity of conclusions drawn from such studies can be questionable. That is, it is not always appropriate to generalise from laboratory research to the real world. Researchers usually belong to a theoretical tradition that determines both the type of research they carry out and the research methods they employ. For example, cognitive psychologists may use lab experiments to investigate mental processes such as memory and problem solving without necessarily considering how such processes might operate in real-life settings.

In criminological psychology, research findings and theories from areas of pure psychology are applied to the questions raised by real-life legal and criminal problems. Figure 1.1 shows the approaches studied in AS-Level Psychology, all of which can be applied to criminological psychology.

These pure psychological approaches could be applied to criminological psychology in a number of ways. For example:

- Cognitive psychology is concerned with the internal mental processes, such as memory and attention, which underlie behaviour. Laboratory research showing that memory is prone to reconstructive memory errors has been applied to the way in which witnesses of crimes may recall events.

The cognitive approach	The learning approach
The social approach	The physiological approach
The developmental approach	The psychodynamic approach

Figure 1.1 **Psychological approaches that can be applied to crime and the legal system**

- Social psychology is concerned with how people interact and the ways in which situational and group influences can affect behaviour. For example, research into conformity has been applied to the way in which juries may reach their verdicts.
- Developmental psychology is concerned with the development of psychological attributes such as morality and personality in childhood and later life. Research into child-rearing styles has been applied as an explanation of criminal behaviour. For example, children whose parents use severe and inconsistent punishments are more likely to become offenders.
- The learning approach is concerned with how the environment can shape our behaviour. Behaviourist principles of learning have been applied to the treatment of offenders, for example, as techniques of behaviour modification.
- Physiological psychology (or biopsychology) is concerned with the influence of the nervous system, hormones and genetics on behaviour. Family and twin studies have been applied to criminal behaviour in order to establish whether genetics play a role in criminality.
- Psychodynamic psychology is concerned with the influence of the unconscious on behaviour and, in particular, how early childhood experiences may have an effect later in life. These ideas have been used by psychologists to assist police with investigations of serial murder and rape. An important question in **offender profiling** is whether the choice of victims is influenced by an earlier episode in the offender's life.

Different types of criminological psychology

The terms criminological, forensic, legal and criminal psychology are often used interchangeably, which can seem confusing. Even within the profession itself, there is debate and confusion over definitions and the boundaries between them. For the purpose of an introduction, it is helpful to look at two different types of criminological psychology: forensic psychology and offender profiling. **Forensic psychology** refers to any psychologist who provides expertise in legal matters. This could include working with offenders in remand centres, prisons and the probation service and providing expert advice on legal procedures such as questioning children or allowing rape victims to provide evidence via a video link. Psychologists involved in offender profiling assist police investigations through developing profiles of the likely characteristics of an offender.

Forensic psychology

There is some debate over what the term forensic psychology actually refers to. It has been taken by some to refer to clinical psychologists who primarily work with offenders. This is not surprising when it is considered that a substantial number of people who call themselves forensic psychologists are clinical psychologists working in the prison and probation services and in special hospitals (Blackburn 1996). In this capacity they may be involved in the assessment and treatment of particular types of offender, for example, sex offenders. They may also play a role in assessing the risks that may be involved when an offender is released. The Committee on Ethical Guidelines for Forensic Psychologists (1991) defines forensic psychology as:

> All forms of professional psychological conduct when acting, with definable foreknowledge, as a psychological expert on explicitly psycho-legal issues, in direct assistance to courts, parties to legal proceedings, correctional and forensic mental health facilities.

Although it is rather longwinded, this definition captures a broader range of activities than the simple definition of clinical psychologists working with offenders. In fact, any kind of psychologist (clinical, educational or social, to name but a few) could be considered to be a forensic psychologist when they apply their expertise to legal questions. According to Blackburn (1996), no matter what kind of background or training the psychologist may have had, all forensic psychology belongs to one of three main strands:

- **Psycho-legal studies** e.g. research into eyewitness testimony or decision making in juries.
- **Criminology** e.g. research into the causes and prevention of crime.
- **Expert evidence** e.g. presenting evidence in court.

What these different strands all have in common is 'the provision of psychological information for the purpose of facilitating a legal decision' (Blackburn 1996). The exact type of information which can be provided in legal matters varies depending on the nature of the case with which the psychologist is involved, but usually falls into one of the following categories; clinical, experimental or advisory (Howard 1981). Figure 1.2 gives an example of how a forensic psychologist can use their clinical expertise to advise the police.

In other cases, forensic psychologists are asked to review evidence or judge the reliability of recall by witnesses. Howard describes one case where three motorcyclists had been charged with dangerous driving resulting in the death of a fourth motorcyclist and pillion passenger. The evidence hinged on the claim of a police officer that he had seen the motorcyclists speeding and taken their numberplates. Is it possible to recall four sets of muddy numberplates, two and a half

---

An adolescent complained to the police that she was receiving frequent indecent telephone calls. Despite continuous monitoring of the calls, none were intercepted. She then alleged her property was being smeared with paint and some items were shown to the police, damaged as described. She became rather belligerent at the police station and considerable time was spent in police inquiries. A psychologist was asked to provide an assessment as to whether or not the girl was manufacturing the evidence in order to satisfy some psychological need. The result of the assessment confirmed the police's suspicions that she had fabricated the incidents.

Source:: Brown (1997)

Figure 1.2 **The forensic psychologist in his/her clinical role**

In a laboratory experiment, 100 participants were asked to identify four sets of number plates. They were presented in a degraded form to mimic real conditions: yards away, two and a half inches high and covered in mud. Results showed a few participants could recall one numberplate and no participants could recall two or more. Despite the doubt cast on the eyewitness testimony of the police officer, the jury was not convinced and all the motorcyclists were convicted.

Source: Brown (1997)

Figure 1.3 **The forensic psychologist in his/her experimental role**

inches high at ninety yards? Psychologists were asked to set up an experiment to test the accuracy of this recall (see Figure 1.3).

Offender profiling

Popular media stereotypes of the criminal psychologist 'getting inside the head' of the criminal (e.g. the film *The Silence of the Lambs* or Granada TV's *Cracker*) are more fiction than reality. In reality, the psychologist examines evidence to look for links between what goes on at the crime scene, and the type of person who may have committed the crime. One of the first recorded uses of offender profiling dates back to an incident in the 1950s when the New York Police Department were unsuccessful in their attempts to apprehend the New York City 'Mad Bomber' after a manhunt. James Brussel, a psychiatrist, became interested in the case and using information provided by the police and his clinical experience, provided a number of predictions about the likely perpetrator (see Figure 1.4). These proved to be incredibly accurate.

Although this was only an 'amateur' profile, in the 1960s the US Federal Bureau of Investigation (FBI) became interested in developing psychological profiles of criminals. Several high-profile cases including Charles Manson and 'The Boston Strangler' involved the successful use of psychological profiles to help narrow down the number of suspects. Encouraged by these and other successes, the FBI decided upon a more systematic and scientific approach. A team of experienced officers with psychological training interviewed rapists and murderers with the aim of understanding the different types of criminal personality.

- Aged between 40 and 50 years old and of Eastern European origin.
- Currently living in Connecticut with either a sister or a maiden aunt.
- Had a poor relationship with his father.
- Loved and got on well with his mother.
- Apt to pay great attention to detail, having a paranoid personality.
- Dresses in double-breasted suits with all the buttons fastened.

The police arrested and charged George Metsky several years after the bombings. As predicted he was living in Connecticut, born in Eastern Europe, aged in his early fifties living with two unmarried sisters and he frequently wore a double-breasted suit. The psychological profile was born.

Source: Brussel (1968)

Figure 1.4 **Brussel's profile of the New York City 'Mad Bomber'**

Their results eventually formed the basis of a national database, the **Violent Criminal Apprehension Program** (VICAP), used to develop psychological profiles of criminals when combined with detailed police reports of the crime scene and the victim.

Profiles are also used by the FBI where there may be a question over the cause of death. When police investigate an unusual death, they may have to determine whether the deceased was murdered or not. This process is rarely straightforward. For example, a murder could have been 'framed', that is, made to look like a suicide. Alternatively, sometimes individuals who commit suicide may try to make it seem as if it was murder. Profilers can help to provide a profile of the deceased, a sort of **psychological autopsy**. An assessment is made of the deceased's personality and life situation, what kind of person they were, what kind of pressure they were under and how they attempted to cope with this pressure.

An example of this kind of work was an investigation by McDowell (1987) into the death of a 27-year-old US Air Force Security Police Sergeant. Events leading up to the death suggested a murder. The last contact with the sergeant was when he radioed base to say he was checking out a pick-up truck and declined back-up. Ten minutes later he was found by another officer with a single gunshot wound to the chest. He was holding his pistol and his handcuffs were nearby with one ratchet open and the other closed. There was no sign of a struggle or any other wounds. How had the sergeant died? Was he shot with his own gun trying to make an arrest? A 'psychological autopsy' carried out by McDowell suggested that the sergeant had staged his own death in order to make it look like a murder (see Figure 1.5).

The sergeant frequently boasted to work colleagues about his macho bravery but in reality the opposite was true. He was in debt, had been arrested for shoplifting, was having marital problems and frequently presented himself at military clinics and hospitals. McDowell proposed that the sergeant had sought to protect his own macho image from the reality of inadequacy and incompetence by a heroic death. His knowledge of forensic and investigative procedures allowed him to stage his own death to look like an authentic murder scene.

Figure 1.5 **Psychological autopsy report (McDowell 1987)**

The remaining chapters of this book will take a more in-depth look at the kind of work carried out by criminological psychologists, such as offender profiling and the treatment of offenders. It will also consider how psychology can be applied to a range of other legal procedures and questions such as how group processes affect the ways in which juries reach decisions and the ways in which police interview suspects.

The following table will help you to work out which chapters of the book are relevant for the specification you are studying.

Table 1.1 Coverage of the different A-Level specifications in this book			
Topics	Specifications		
The nature and measurement of offending	Edexcel	AQA – B	OCR
What is a criminal?	✔	✔	
Measuring crime		✔	✔
Victimisation			✔
Biologically oriented explanations of criminal behaviour			
Constitutional theories of criminality		✔	✔
Genetic research into criminality			✔
Biological research into criminality			✔
Eysenck's personality theory		✔	✔
Psychologically oriented explanations of criminal behaviour			
Psychoanalytical theories of crime		✔	✔
Learning theories of crime	✔	✔	✔
Cognitive theories of crime		✔	✔
Social theories of crime	✔	✔	✔
The police and crime			
Policing			✔
Interviewing			✔
Negotiation			✔
Offender profiling			
Principles of offender profiling	✔	✔	✔
Biases and pitfalls in offender profiling	✔	✔	✔
The psychology of testimony			
Cognitive processes and testimony	✔		✔
Attribution theory and bias in eyewitness testimony	✔		
Identification of suspects and events			✔
Aids to witness recall and recognition	✔		✔

The psychology of the courtroom			
Trial procedures			✔
Jury processes	✔		✔
Child witnesses			✔
Punishing, treating and preventing crime			
Imprisonment		✔	✔
Non-custodial sentencing		✔	✔
Psychological treatment programmes	✔	✔	✔
Crime prevention	✔		✔

2

The nature and measurement of offending

What is a criminal?
Measuring crime
Victimisation

The scientific study of offenders and offending requires some agreement between practitioners about which people and which acts should be studied. This chapter begins with a discussion of different definitions of 'criminal' and goes on to assess different ways of measuring the extent of crime within a given society. Some consideration is given to factors that appear to influence an individual's chances of becoming either a criminal or a victim of crime. Finally, there is a discussion of why people tend to have a fear of crime that is disproportionate to their chances of being victimised.

WHAT IS A CRIMINAL?

It might seem an easy task to define what a criminal is, namely, a person who breaks the judicial laws of the society in which they live. It might follow from this that criminological psychology should study only such individuals. Unfortunately, things are not as simple as this. It is a matter of some debate which people should be studied by criminological psychologists. In order to understand more fully the nature of this problem it is useful to consider two possible approaches to defining 'criminal', referred to here as the 'legalistic' and 'deviance' approaches.

Progress exercise

In order to conduct research into criminal behaviour, it is first necessary to define what a criminal is. It might be suggested that a criminal is anyone who breaks the law. Try to identify some potential problems with defining criminality in this way.

The legalistic approach

The simplest definition of a criminal is a person who transgresses the laws of their society. Unfortunately, this definition is over-inclusive: it defines as 'criminal' many individuals who would not normally be considered as such. According to many writers almost everyone has broken the law at some time in their life. For example, every time someone uses their work telephone for personal business they may technically be guilty of breaking the law (Ainsworth 2000). If we accept that all such people are to be classified as criminals then it follows that virtually everyone is a criminal. One alternative to this is to define criminals in terms of having been convicted of a crime by the state. It follows from this that criminological psychology should study only those people who have a criminal record. This is also unsatisfactory but this time because the definition is under-inclusive. In many cases the person responsible for a particular crime escapes detection. If detected they may not be prosecuted and if prosecuted they may not be convicted. Thus, many people who have committed criminal acts would not be considered appropriate for study by criminological psychologists if the definition of criminal was restricted to those convicted of crimes. There are additional problems with the legalistic approach. First, the population of convicted offenders will inevitably contain a number of people who have been wrongly convicted of crimes. Second, those who have been convicted of the crimes they have committed are, in a manner of speaking, 'unsuccessful' criminals.

If criminological psychology was restricted to the study of such individuals it might well be using a sample biased towards those offenders with attributes (e.g. lower intelligence) which made it more likely that they would be caught.

The deviance approach

Some writers (e.g. Sellin 1938) suggest that the appropriate object of study for criminological psychology is 'deviance' or 'antisocial behaviour', of which legally defined crime is just a part. It follows from this that criminological psychology should study those people who behave in antisocial ways. Given the problems with the 'legalistic' viewpoint this might seem more satisfactory. Unfortunately, the classification of behaviour as deviant or antisocial is notoriously subjective. An act may be considered pro- or antisocial depending on one's point of view. For example, a person who defaced a building to draw attention to the oppression of a particular group of people might be considered to be acting antisocially by the owner of the building but pro-socially by those sympathetic to the cause being represented. This being the case it is difficult to see how consensus could be achieved amongst researchers about which acts they should be studying.

Blackburn (1993) makes several useful recommendations to help clarify this debate. First, he suggests that criminal behaviour be defined in terms of the conscious breaking of rules. This allows a connection to be drawn between conduct problems early in life and 'official' criminality later. Second, he states that the psychological investigation of criminal behaviour should centre on crime as legally defined, since this at least offers a mutually agreed framework for researchers. However, third, he states that researchers must also consider behaviour which has not been legally defined as criminal since, in many cases, legally defined crime is connected with 'antisocial' behaviour which is not in itself considered criminal by the authorities. Whilst this does not offer a resolution to the debates described above it does at least provide an indication of a productive way forward for the psychological investigation of criminality.

Variables associated with criminality

Surveys in which people are asked about their own criminal activities, particularly those of young people, indicate that the **prevalence of criminality** (i.e. the number of people committing crimes) is far higher than many people assume (see below). It could even be suggested that petty crime, rather than being an aberration, is actually a normative activity amongst certain groups in the population. However, notwithstanding the fact that most people will break the law at some point in their lives (see above), a minority of people commits the majority of offences and certain groups are over-represented in the offender population. Research into the social and familial correlates of crime can help lead to an understanding of why certain individuals are more likely than others to become criminals. Some of the variables associated with criminality are socio-economic status, age and gender.

Socio-economic status

It is widely believed that there is an inverse relationship between **socio-economic status** (SES) and criminality. That is, people from low-SES backgrounds are over-represented amongst the population of offenders. For example, stereotypical views of 'the criminal' frequently include the notion that they are working class (Dane and Wrightsman 1982). Whilst some research supports the idea that low SES is associated with criminality, the relationship between offending and SES is weaker than many people assume. One issue that arose from earlier studies of the relationship between SES and criminality was that the relationship appeared much stronger for official measures of offending than for self-report measures. This finding may reflect bias in the way that people from different social backgrounds are processed by the criminal justice system, as some studies have shown that low SES can militate against a defendant at trial. Rutter and Giller (1983) found a small correlation between SES and crime but it is open to question what the origin of this is. Sociological theorists favour explanations based around the relative lack of opportunities open to people from low-SES backgrounds, whilst more psychologically oriented theorists tend to indicate the learning of delinquent values from family and peers as possible explanations. A fuller account of different explanations of criminal behaviour is given in Chapters 3 and 4.

Age

Age seems to be an important correlate of offending. As discussed above, surveys of young people have indicated that criminal acts are relatively common amongst this group. Generally, offending commences in adolescence, rises steadily and peaks around the age of 18, falling sharply thereafter. However, there are marked variations if different types of crime are accounted for. Property-related crimes such as theft follow the pattern just described whereas crimes like fraud and embezzlement are far more likely to be committed by older adults (Steffenmeister et al. 1989). This mainly reflects a difference in opportunity since teenagers and young adults are far less likely to find themselves in a position to commit offences like embezzlement. Explanations of the age distribution of crime draw on both biological and social perspectives. For example, violent offending in males may correlate with **testosterone** levels, which peak at around 18 years of age. Testosterone has been shown to exert an influence on aggression (Kalat 1998). The decline in property offending after the age of 21 could be explained in terms of individuals 'settling down' and entering stable relationships and employment.

Gender

Criminal statistics consistently report a far higher prevalence of offending amongst males than females. Again, this varies by type of offence, so whilst the vast majority of burglaries, robberies and violent crimes are committed by men, gender differences are less marked for theft and fraud. There are a number of possible reasons for this. One is that gender differences in offending reflect constitutional differences between males and females. This is more likely to be the case for personal and violent crimes where gender differences are most marked. However, an alternative possibility is that gender differences in criminal behaviour reflect differences in the socialisation of men and women. Box (1983) found that criminality in women correlated with the degree of female subordination and powerlessness within society. It could be that societies which stress a more 'traditional' female role restrict the opportunities available to women to become involved in criminal activity. It is likely that biology and socialisation interact in complex ways to produce gender differences in violent crimes.

However, the reduced gender differences for non-violent crimes such as cheque fraud suggest a social, rather than a biological explanation. It seems probable that women have fewer opportunities to commit certain types of crime, as they are less likely to become involved in criminal subcultures and gangs. The social explanation is further supported by the observation that gender differences in crime have been narrowing for some time.

MEASURING CRIME

Just as it might seem simple at the outset to define what a criminal is, it might also seem relatively straightforward to measure how much crime there is. Surely it is just a matter of counting how many crimes occur? Once again, matters are not that simple. The **crime rate** of a given country or area is calculated by counting how many offences occur and dividing by the number of people who live there. The problem is, there are a number of ways of counting crimes and they tend not to agree on how much crime there is. The three main sources of information about the extent of crime are official crime statistics; victimisation surveys such as the **British Crime Survey**; and offender surveys. Each of these sources of information has its strengths and weaknesses but all of them distort the 'true' figure of crime to some extent.

Official crime statistics

In the UK the official crime rate is calculated on the basis of crime figures returned to the Home Office by the various regional police forces. These are compiled and published annually in the Home Office publication *Criminal Statistics*. It is widely agreed that the Home Office statistics heavily underestimate the true extent of crime. There are a number of reasons for this. First, many crimes are not reported to the police. Often the crime is not considered 'serious enough' by the victim to warrant reporting. Some victims of crime may believe that there is little the police can do or that it is more appropriate to deal with the matter personally (Hough and Mayhew 1983). Additionally, some crimes (e.g. drug dealing) involve a 'willing victim' and are highly unlikely to be reported. Hollin (1989) also points out that, in certain cases, the victim may not realise that a crime has been committed, possibly because they did not notice (for example, minor acts of vandalism, whilst criminal, may be regarded as accidental by the victim). For all these reasons many of the crimes that happen are not brought to the attention of the police. It should be stressed that unreported crimes are not always offences considered too trivial to report and that a proportion of unreported crime would be classified as serious.

Even if a crime is reported to the police it does not automatically follow that it will appear on official statistics. The police have a great deal of discretion over whether crimes reported to them are recorded as such and there are a number of reasons why a reported crime may not become a recorded crime. The police may decide that the report is a mistake or that there is insufficient evidence that a crime has been committed. Alternatively, the victim may withdraw their complaint, in which case the incident will be written off as 'no crime'. There is considerable variation in the policies adopted by different police forces on the recording of crime and this can result in apparent variations in the crime rate between regions. Ainsworth (2000) gives the example of the violent crime figures for 1997–1998. These data showed an apparently huge rise in violent offences in the West Midlands and Greater Manchester of 33.3 per cent and 49.4 per cent respectively. Although these figures caused a great deal of concern amongst members of the public, Povey and Prime (1998) suggest that they came about because of improved crime recording rather than a leap in the actual number of offences committed. To reiterate, the official crime figures have a tendency to under-represent the actual incidence of crime. This occurs because some crimes are not reported and because not all reported crimes are recorded as such. This situation results in a **dark figure** of unrecorded crime. In order to estimate the size of the dark figure, other ways of measuring crime must be employed. In the UK this usually means using data from **victimisation surveys**, chiefly the British Crime Survey.

Victimisation surveys

In a victimisation survey, rather than relying on official figures to estimate the incidence of crime, a large sample of the population are questioned about their experience of crime. A number of countries carry out large-scale victimisation surveys. In the USA the annual National Crime Survey (NCS) surveys the experience of crime in 132,000 households across the country. Similar surveys are carried out in Australia and the Scandinavian countries (Hollin 1989). In the UK the British Crime Survey (BCS) is the most generally cited source of information about the true extent of crime. It involves a large number of households (around 11,000 in England and Wales and 5,000 in Scotland) selected from the electoral roll. One person aged 16 years or over is questioned from each household about whether he or she has been a victim of crime, the details of the crime (if any) and their attitudes towards crime. This makes the BCS not only a useful alternative to the official crime statistics but also a valuable source of data on attitudes towards and fear of crime (see below).

The British Crime Survey has consistently revealed a far higher number of crimes than that reported by the Home Office statistics. For example, the 1998 BCS found that just a quarter of crimes reported in the survey were also recorded by the police. This is because less than half of the crimes recorded by the BCS were reported to the police and, of these, about half were recorded by the police as crimes (Mirrlees-Black et al. 1998). However, it should be pointed out that much of the dark figure revealed by the BCS consists of relatively minor offences resulting in little or no personal loss or injury (for example, vandalism and burglary without loss). If the BCS and the official statistics are compared, similar estimates are given for the incidence of more serious crimes, although it should be noted that a significant proportion (around a third) of serious offences such as wounding, burglary and robbery go unreported to the authorities (Mirrlees-Black et al. 1998). However, it should not be supposed that the BCS provides a completely accurate figure of the extent of crime in the UK. Some of the offences recorded by the BCS, such as common assault, are no longer officially defined as crimes by the UK authorities. Additionally, the BCS focuses on offences against property and the person and does not attempt to measure the incidence of certain crimes (e.g. fraud) so it provides no information about the incidence of these and some other offences.

Offender surveys

An alternative way of gathering information about the extent of crime is to focus on the perpetrators rather than the victims. This could be important as it can help to guide estimates not only of the **incidence of crime** (that is, the number of offences committed) but also the **prevalence of crime** (the number of people committing offences). Since fluctuations in the crime rate can be the result of changes in both incidence and prevalence, surveys of offenders may be particularly useful in helping to explain apparent changes in the crime rate. A number of offender surveys were carried out in the UK in the 1960s and 1970s. Hollin (1989) cites a survey carried out by Belson (1975) as a fairly typical example: 1,445 boys aged between 13 and 16 were sampled from a random selection of London households. Interviews revealed that around 70 per cent of those sampled had stolen from a shop whilst around 17 per cent had been involved with stealing from private premises. Since these data are for offences that would normally lead to prosecution it seems that this survey also supports the view that a large dark figure of unreported crime exists. More recently the Home Office has gathered data on offending amongst young people as part of its *Youth Lifestyles* survey. The 1998 survey indicated that 26 per cent of young men and 11 per cent of young women had committed a criminal offence in the previous year. Of these, only 12 per cent reported that they had been cautioned or prosecuted. Although it is likely that some of the remainder had come to the attention of the police these data also support the conclusion that the dark figure of unrecorded crime may be many times the actual reported figure. Like official and victimisation statistics, data from offender surveys can be subject to criticism. Although self-reports of offending seem to agree quite well with other measures such as peer reports and police records (Hindelang et al. 1981), there may be problems with how the sample is obtained. For example, if respondents are surveyed at school then persistent truants may be missed. Since it is likely that these individuals will be involved in committing the more serious types of offence this may lead to an underestimation of the true prevalence of offending.

To conclude, it is impossible, based on the available information, to provide an accurate estimate of how much crime is actually committed. All the available methods for gathering this information tend to underestimate the incidence of crime. This is particularly the case for the official crime statistics based on police records. However, it should be stressed that the majority of the dark figure of unrecorded crime is accounted for by relatively minor and 'victimless' offences.

Progress exercise

What are the strengths and weaknesses of the different ways of gathering crime statistics? Which method is likely to give the most accurate estimate of (a) the incidence and (b) the prevalence of crime?

VICTIMISATION

This section will give an overview of the factors that appear to influence victimisation, which will then be compared to people's reported fear of crime. Data from the BCS suggest a range of factors that affect the likelihood of someone being victimised and it appears that different socio-economic groups are affected by different types of crime. The British Crime Survey is particularly useful because it gathers information not just on the extent of crime but also on people's attitudes towards it. This allows a comparison to be made between people's fear of crime and their actual chances of becoming a victim. One consistent finding from the BCS is that, generally, people's fear of crime is exaggerated compared to their actual chances of becoming a victim.

Burglary

One of the major factors influencing burglary victimisation is geographical location. Certain areas suffer more heavily from this crime than others. Additionally, factors within a geographical location, such as type of property, also exert an influence. The 1998 BCS identified the following factors as contributing to an increased risk of victimisation for a household: inner city location; located on a council estate; not located in a cul-de-sac; in the north of England. Some demographic variables were also found to be relevant. For example, a household is more at risk if the head of the household is young, unemployed or on a low income or a single parent. Many of these variables overlap and their influence becomes more obvious if they are combined. Thus for low-income households in an inner city area the chances of being burgled are almost 20 per cent, compared with just 2.3 per cent for older households in a rural area.

Vehicle theft

Whilst for burglary the highest risk is run by the lowest income group, for vehicle theft the reverse is true. Ainsworth (2000) cites a number of possible reasons for this. Higher income households are more likely to own two or more vehicles, meaning that they run a higher risk of one vehicle being stolen. Additionally, they tend to own more valuable (and hence desirable) vehicles and are more mobile, meaning they are more likely to leave their vehicles in high-risk locations such as car parks.

Violent crime

Throughout the 1990s the risk in the general population of becoming a victim of violent crime was around 5 per cent (e.g. 4.7 per cent in 1997). The greatest proportion of this is accounted for by relatively minor violent acts such as common assault (Mirrlees-Black et al. 1998). However, there are large variations in vulnerability. In general, people are more likely to be the victims of violent crime if they are young, a single parent, are unemployed and living in rented accommodation. Additional risk factors include living in a flat or terraced house and going out frequently. Once again, many of these factors are related and large differences can be seen if they are combined. Thus, people in rented accommodation in an inner city area have almost a 19 per cent risk of victimisation compared to less than two per cent for rural owner-occupiers.

The effects of victimisation

It is almost inevitable that a person will experience some degree of distress as a result of being victimised, especially if the crime is a violent one. Kahn (1984) identifies a large number of possible responses to victimisation including depression, anxiety, paranoia, shock and anger. Davis and Friedman (1985) found that 75 per cent of a sample of burglary victims reported psychological symptoms, including anxiety

Progress exercise

Even if you have never been a victim of crime, it is likely that you know someone who has. Try to identify some of the ways in which a person might be affected by victimisation. You may find it helpful to divide the effects of victimisation into cognitive, emotional and behavioural effects.

and disturbed sleep, three weeks after the offence. Not surprisingly, one of the main determinants of a victim's reaction is the seriousness of the crime. However, it should be noted that people vary in the extent to which they are adversely affected by victimisation. Two important variables which affect how a person will be affected by victimisation are belief in a just world and locus of control.

Belief in a just world

Whilst some people may consider that victims of crime are just 'unlucky', others may believe that, if precautions are taken, one need never become a victim. Lerner (1970) calls the belief that the world is a fair place in which people generally deserve the things that happen to them the '**just world hypothesis**'. The extent of a person's belief in a just world can affect how they view victims of crime and how they cope with victimisation themselves. Those who believe in a just world may benefit from doing so by avoiding anxiety about being victimised themselves. They may reason that, since people generally get what they deserve, anyone who has taken the appropriate precautions will never be victimised. However, people with a strong belief in a just world are likely to be hit harder by victimisation as they will find it more difficult to understand why they have been singled out. A person who believes that they will inevitably be victimised will probably cope better with the experience of victimisation than a person who believes they have taken every possible precaution and hence were invulnerable (Ainsworth 2000). Belief in a just world can also affect how victims of crime are perceived in a judicial context. This issue is discussed further in Chapter 7.

Locus of control

Personality variables also affect how a person adjusts to the experience of victimisation. One important personality variable is **locus of control**, or the extent to which a person believes they are in charge of their own destiny (Rotter 1966). Individuals with an internal locus of control tend to believe that the things which happen to them are largely the result of their own actions, whereas those with an external locus of control tend to see themselves as victims of circumstances. It should be noted that locus of control represents a continuum of beliefs rather than two distinct types of people: a person may be strongly internal, strongly external or somewhere in between. People with a strongly internal locus of control are likely to respond more negatively to the experience of victimisation, presumably for the same reasons that people who believe in a just world are more affected. However, those with a strongly internal locus of control are more likely to take steps following victimisation to avoid being affected by crime again. People with a strongly external locus of control are less likely to believe that any action they take will make a difference to what happens to them in the future.

Fear of crime

Surveys like the BCS have consistently shown that people tend to overestimate the incidence of crime. This being the case, people tend to have a fear of crime that is disproportionate compared to their actual chances of being victimised. It appears that, for certain crimes, this exaggeration is actually greatest amongst those who are least likely to become victims. For example, the elderly are often reported to be most fearful of being assaulted but run a risk of only 0.2 per cent (women) and 1 per cent (men) of being victimised. Conversely, young men between 16 and 24 typically report the least fear of victimisation yet the level of assault victimisation for this group is around 20 per cent (Mirrlees-Black et al. 1998). The BCS also indicates that people tend to believe that the crime rate is rising, even when it has actually fallen.

The main reason for the public's misperception of their chances of being victimised seems to be that they gather information about crime from media sources such as newspapers or television programmes that do not accurately reflect the reality of crime. News media have a tendency to focus on unusual and horrific events. Murders receive extensive coverage although murder, in the UK, remains an extremely rare crime. In order to attract audience share, news media will tend to focus on sensational and horrific crimes even if these are the exception rather than the norm. Although news media do report crime statistics such as the BCS, they typically focus on the aspects of the report which report a rise in victimisation and pay little attention to reported falls in the crime rate (Ainsworth 2000). The result is that the public are constantly exposed to accounts of murder, rape and abduction and may come to believe that the frequency with which these are reported reflects the likelihood of members of the public being victimised in this way (**deviance amplification**). The same is true of fictionalised crime in television programmes, which regularly feature statistically rare crimes such as violent attacks on strangers. Cumberbatch (1989) estimates that, although the general risk of being victimised is quite low, the average person will be exposed to around 7,000 crimes a year by media sources. In the light of this figure, it is not surprising that people tend to have an inaccurate perception of the likelihood that they will be affected by crime.

Chapter summary

There is considerable debate over which individuals and acts should be studied by criminological psychologists. However, most researchers agree that research should concentrate mainly on criminals as legally defined. Official statistics, victimisation and offender surveys are all ways of measuring crime. They have a tendency to underestimate the extent of crime (particularly official statistics) and it appears that there is a dark figure of unrecorded criminal activity. Demographic variables such as socio-economic status, age and gender influence the likelihood of an individual becoming both an offender and a victim. Other variables also influence victimisation, particularly geographical location. Several variables affect the way individuals respond to victimisation. People with a strong belief in a just world or a highly internal locus of control are likely to be more adversely affected. Generally, people have an exaggerated fear of being victimised and believe that the incidence of crime is far greater that it actually is. The main reason for this is that they obtain information about crime from media sources that exaggerate its incidence.

Further reading

P.B. Ainsworth (2000) *Psychology and Crime: Myths and Reality*. Harlow: Pearson Education. Chapter 1 contains a very readable account of measures of offending and fear of crime.

C. Mirrlees-Black et al. (1998) *The 1998 British Crime Survey: England and Wales*. Home Office Research, Development and Statistics Directorate. An excellent summary of the 1998 BCS. Available on the web at www.homeoffice.gov.uk/rds/index.htm

3

Biologically oriented explanations of criminal behaviour

- Constitutional theories of criminality
- Recent genetic research into criminality
- Biological research into criminality
- Eysenck's personality theory

One of the main problems faced by criminological psychology is explaining why people become criminals. This knowledge might open the way to preventing crime through psychological or other interventions. This chapter and the next will examine a number of different theories that aim to explain why some people become criminals. The theories considered in this chapter have been grouped together as 'biologically oriented' as they are all based around the idea that criminality is the effect of genetic or biological characteristics of the individual. However, within this general theme there is great variation in the kinds of theories which have been put forward. This chapter will first consider two early theories which suggested that criminal tendencies were inherited, before moving on to a discussion of more recent genetic research and a consideration of the role of brain abnormalities in criminality. Finally, Eysenck's personality theory will be discussed. Although this originates in the psychometric, rather than the biological tradition in psychology, it is included here because Eysenck argued that personality has a biological basis.

CONSTITUTIONAL THEORIES OF CRIMINALITY

The earliest theories of criminality tended to be based on the idea that it is an inherited tendency. However, it must be stressed that many early theorists were prepared to consider that the environment also played a part in producing criminal behaviour. The two theories that will be discussed in this section are Lombroso's theory of criminal types, generally considered the founding theory of modern criminology, and Sheldon's theory of somatotypes, which suggests that criminality is associated with bodily build.

Lombroso's theory of criminal types

The idea that criminality is a heritable, constitutional variable was first advanced in a systematic way by Lombroso in the late nineteenth century. Lombroso (1876) claimed that criminals constituted a biologically distinct class of people united by a tendency to exhibit 'throwback' or primitive characteristics: strong jaws, heavy brows and lower than average intelligence. Lombroso, who was influenced by the work of phrenologists (who thought that a person's psychological characteristics could be 'read' from the shape of their skull), suggested that different subtypes of criminal could be identified through their physical characteristics. For example, murderers were said to have bloodshot eyes, strong jaws and curly hair whereas sex offenders were characterised by thick lips and projecting ears. Initially, Lombroso claimed that these characteristics were inherited and hence suggested that criminals are 'born' and not 'made'. However, in later writings he suggested that only about one third of criminals had directly inherited their criminality. The remainder, he claimed, had become criminal due to association with criminals (acquired degeneracy) and due to a number of other factors such as poor education.

Evaluation of Lombroso's theory

Lombroso's ideas provoked a great deal of debate at the time, feeding, as they did, into more general discussions taking place about the problem of the 'criminal classes' (Garland 1997). However, it is clear that his work was fundamentally flawed for a number of reasons. First, he did not compare the criminals he studied with a group of non-criminal controls in order to establish whether the characteristics he identified as 'criminal' occurred in the non-criminal population. Second, he included in his sample a large number of people who would today be classified as suffering from a psychological disorder of some sort and hence he confused criminality with psychopathology. Although Lombroso's theories can be dismissed on the basis of such objections, his work was not without value. Arguably, Lombroso, with his insistence on empirical evidence and scientific method (however weakly applied), was responsible for shifting the study of criminality away from the realm of moral and philosophical discussion and into the domain of scientific research. As such he is regarded by many researchers as 'the father of modern criminology' (Schafer 1976).

Sheldon's theory of somatotypes

An alternative theory of criminality which stresses the importance of physical appearance was put forward by Sheldon (1949). Sheldon attempted to link criminal behaviour to bodily build or **somatotype**. According to Sheldon, there are three basic body types: endomorphs (fat), ectomorphs (thin) and mesomorphs (muscular). Sheldon claimed that somatotype was linked to personality and temperament so that ectomorphs tend to be relaxed and hedonistic, endomorphs restrained and solitary and mesomorphs energetic and adventurous (Blackburn 1993). Sheldon reasoned that the temperament of mesomorphs might lead to them being more likely to become involved in criminal activity. It is important to stress that Sheldon believed that pure somatotypes were rare and that most people represented a blending of different degrees of each type. However, he nonetheless suggested that a person's degree of mesomorphy could predict their degree of criminality.

Evaluation of Sheldon's theory

Sheldon obtained evidence using studies in which the somatotypes of college students and delinquents were assessed from photographs. Each photograph was rated for mesomorphy on a scale of 1 (lowest) to 7 (highest). He found that the delinquents had a generally higher degree of mesomorphy than the college students, a mean rating of 4.6 compared to 3.8. A follow-up study of Sheldon's delinquent sample by Hartl et al. (1982) found that those who went on to be the most seriously criminal had a mean mesomorphy rating of 5.0. These results, then, support the idea that mesomorphy is associated with delinquency. Other studies of the relationship between mesomorphy and delinquency have produced mixed support for Sheldon's hypothesis. Sutherland (1951) criticised the way that Sheldon selected his sample of delinquents. He did not use legal criteria (i.e. his 'delinquents' had not been officially defined as such). When Sheldon's data were re-analysed using official criteria for delinquency the association between mesomorphy and delinquency was no longer present.

However, research has found a significant association between mesomorphy and criminal tendencies in samples of Borstal boys (Gibbens 1963) and female delinquents (Epps and Parnell 1952). Blackburn (1993) concludes that, although many such studies suffer from methodological problems, particularly in the way that meso-morphy is assessed, there is a degree of support for the idea that criminality and bodily build are linked. What remains unclear is why this should be so. Amongst the possibilities identified by Blackburn are that mesomorphy may reflect higher testosterone levels and hence higher aggressiveness (Hartl et al. 1982). Alternatively, peer groups and the judicial system may react differently to people with a muscular, tough appearance. For example, they may be more likely to be drawn into delinquent activities and perhaps to be treated more harshly by the judicial system. What is clear from the research on somatotype and its relationship with criminality is that mesomorphy is neither necessary nor sufficient for criminal behaviour and therefore psychol-ogists must look elsewhere in their search for general explanations of criminal behaviour.

RECENT GENETIC RESEARCH INTO CRIMINALITY

Lombroso's and Sheldon's theories are similar in that they attempt to locate the causes of criminal behaviour within some sort of 'criminal gene' or single inherited characteristic. Recent genetic research has moved away from this rather simplistic idea and now concentrates on identifying possible genetic *contributions* to criminality. The three main research approaches used in this area are family, twin and adoption studies.

Family studies

If criminality has a heritable component then we might expect it to run in families. That is, criminal parents will produce a higher than average number of criminal offspring. This tendency had been noted at the time of Lombroso's research and a large number of studies support the suggestion that people born of a criminal parent run a higher risk of becoming criminals themselves. For example, Osborn and West (1979) report that around 40 per cent of the sons of criminal fathers go on to get a criminal record compared to only 13 per cent of the sons of non-criminal fathers. West (1982) and Cloninger et al. (1978) report similar findings.

Although early researchers argued that such evidence strongly hinted at a genetic contribution to criminality it is clear that such a conclusion is unjustified. There are a number of other possibilities besides genetics that might explain why criminal families tend to produce criminal offspring. First, a correlation cannot be used to prove that two variables are causally linked. Although there is a correlation between the criminality of fathers and sons, this might be due to a third variable which affects both, such as social class, unemployment or poor education (Hollin 1989). Second, criminal behaviour might be transmitted from one generation to the next by other means, such as social learning or the reinforcement of antisocial values. Thus, the key problem with family studies is that they do not allow us to separate out the effects of genetics from the effects of the environment.

Twin studies

An alternative methodology that attempts to avoid this problem is the twin study. In one kind of twin study, **monozygotic** (identical) and **dizygotic** (non-identical) twin pairs are compared. The rationale is that, if each member of a twin pair has a roughly identical environment, any difference in the average similarity of MZ and DZ twins must be due to a genetic influence. Specifically, if there is a genetic contribution to the characteristic being studied, MZ would be expected to be more similar than DZ twins. The conventional way of expressing the degree of similarity between twin pairs is by using concordance rates. A concordance rate is the degree to which members of a twin pair display the same characteristics, expressed as a percentage. Therefore, if it is claimed that MZ twins are 50 per cent concordant for criminality this means that in 50 per cent of MZ twin pairs studied, both twins showed evidence of criminality whereas in the remaining 50 per cent of twin pairs, only one of the twins showed signs of criminality.

A number of early twin studies claimed results that supported the genetic hypothesis. However, these tended to be flawed, as, in the absence of genetic tests, there was no reliable way of deciding whether twin pairs were mono- or dizygotic. Studies that are more recent have found less obvious differences between MZ and DZ concordance rates. However, they apparently support the suggestion of a genetic contribution to criminality. Christiansen (1977) studied all the twin pairs (3,586) from the Danish islands, thereby bypassing one of the standard objections to twin studies, their typically small sample size. Christiansen found concordance rates of 35 per cent (MZ) and 13 per cent (DZ) for male twins and 21 per cent (MZ) and 8 per cent (DZ) for female. Dalgaard and Kringlen (1976) carried out a similar study in Norway and found concordance rates of 26 per cent (MZ) and 15 per cent (DZ).

These findings support the idea that criminal tendencies are to some degree inherited. However, a number of important points should be made. First, the concordance rates, with a maximum of 35 per cent, were rather low, indicating a substantial environmental contribution to criminal behaviour. Second, it is possible that higher concordance rates in MZ twins reflect the fact that they typically share a closer relationship and, because they look very similar, may be treated more similarly than DZ twins are. In addition to this, it is possible for a DZ twin pair to consist of male and female offspring whereas MZ twins are, by definition, the same sex. The fact that males are generally more likely to engage in criminal behaviour may explain the lower concordance rate in DZ twins. In order to decide the issue it would be necessary to study MZ twins reared apart. Unfortunately, this research design has been little used in the study of criminality (Hollin 1989).

Adoption studies

Adoption studies, as the name suggests, examine people who have been born to one set of parents and raised by another. The rationale behind this is that where there is a strong genetic influence on behaviour, adoptees will share more characteristics with their biological than their adoptive parents. Alternatively, if environmental influences on the characteristic being examined are more important then there will be a greater degree of similarity between a child and its adoptive parents. Crowe (1972) found that, where the biological mother of an adoptee had a criminal record, so did nearly 50 per cent of adoptees by the age of eighteen. In the group of children whose mothers had no criminal record, the corresponding figure was only 5 per cent. Hutchings and Mednick (1975) examined criminality in both biological and adoptive fathers. If both had a criminal record, 36.2 per cent of sons also became criminals. When only the biological father was criminal 21.4 per cent did so and when only the adoptive father had a criminal record so did 11.5 per cent of the sons. When neither father had a criminal record, 10.5 per cent of sons went on to get one.

Both of these studies illustrate the importance of genetics in the development of criminal behaviour. Hutchings and Mednick's study also highlights the importance of the environment as it demonstrates the contribution made by the criminality of the adoptive father. One important mediating factor in the inheritance of criminal tendencies may be alcoholism. Bohman et al. (1982) found that when the biological father was alcoholic, the son also tended to be. These individuals tended to be convicted of violent crimes. Criminality of biological sons still correlated with criminality in non-alcoholic fathers, but the crimes tended to be petty and non-violent. These studies suggest that criminal tendencies are, to some extent, passed on from biological parent to offspring. However, there is still need for caution in ascribing this to genetic factors. Stott (1982) points out that the prenatal environment may also influence how the child subsequently develops. Criminal convictions are associated with lower socio-economic status. This, in turn, is associated with a higher degree of stress on the mother of a developing child. Since stress during pregnancy is linked to a variety of developmental problems, including behaviour disorders, it could be that adopted children of criminal parents are at a higher risk of criminality because of problems incurred during prenatal development.

Finally, like family and twin studies, adoption studies have certain limitations that should be considered. First, children who are adopted may be placed in environments similar to that from which they were adopted. Second, some children are adopted months or even years after birth, raising the possibility that their early life experiences may contribute to later criminality.

What are the problems with research which suggests that criminality has a genetic component? You may wish to consider ethical as well as methodological issues.

Evaluation of genetic research

Methodological problems notwithstanding, the evidence above suggests that genetics may contribute in some ways to criminality. What is less clear is how this could be the case. As Ainsworth (2000) points out, we are unlikely ever to find a specific gene that causes someone to become a certain type of criminal. The variety of different types of crime and the fact that legal definitions of criminal acts change over time mean that it would be pointless to try to identify a gene for, say, burglary or financial fraud. However, there remains the possibility that certain heritable behavioural traits, such as aggressiveness, contribute directly to violent crime.

Ainsworth also notes that genetic theories of offending have difficulty explaining why the pattern of offending typically changes over the life-span, rising to a peak in the early 20s and declining or changing thereafter. One way to avoid this problem is to avoid thinking of the inheritance of criminality *per se*. It may be a far more useful approach to consider that certain general behavioural *tendencies* might be transmitted genetically (not a particularly radical suggestion). If the individual is exposed to a particular set of individual, social and cultural factors, these tendencies may result in the person committing acts that their society defines as criminal. For example, an individual with a genetic predisposition to alcoholism is unlikely to become alcoholic in a culture in which exposure to alcohol is highly limited. In such a context, they are unlikely to drink alcohol and hence commit criminal acts associated with alcohol abuse. In other words, criminality may result from an interaction between genetic tendencies and a particular environment.

BIOLOGICAL RESEARCH INTO CRIMINALITY

Few, if any, psychologists would propose that all examples of criminal behaviour can be linked to abnormalities of brain functioning. However, there is some support for the idea that certain types of crime, particularly those involving violence, may be related to brain dysfunction of some sort. Research in this area has tended to focus on persistent, violent offenders, particularly those classified as **psychopaths**.

Structural brain abnormalities

One recent approach to understanding the biology of psychopathy has been taken by Mitchell and Blair (1999). They suggest that the underlying problem in psychopathy is a lack of empathy with others. Following the work of the ethologist Lorenz, they propose that humans have a mechanism similar to that of social animals for terminating aggressive attacks when the victim shows a submissive signal. Many animal species avoid serious injury when conflict occurs between **conspecifics** by means of an innate system whereby a certain submissive behavioural signal (e.g. showing the neck) will terminate the aggressor's attack. In humans, the function of a submissive signal might be served by a sad or fearful facial expression. The response to such expressions is feelings of empathy, which terminate an aggressive attack. Blair et al. (1999) showed that a brain structure called the **amygdala**, known to be involved in emotion, increases its activity when a person is shown pictures of a sad face. The degree of activity in the amygdala was related to the degree of sadness of the face. Mitchell and Blair suggest that, in psychopaths, the functioning of the amygdala is impaired so that they do not respond to empathy-triggering signals from other people. Mitchell and Blair do not suggest that amygdala dysfunction in itself causes people to become psychopaths. Rather, they propose that a dysfunctional amygdala represents a biological *risk factor* for psychopathy. Amygdala dysfunction affects the person by making it more difficult for them to become socialised in the usual way. Whether or not a person develops the disorder will be the outcome of a developmental process influenced by a range of other variables.

In evaluating biological research into criminality it should be restated that it is highly unlikely that all or even most crime is caused by biological abnormalities. However, it is possible that brain

37

dysfunction may, in some cases, lead to behavioural tendencies which may result in certain types of criminal behaviour, especially those involving violence. Many psychologists feel uncomfortable pointing to genetic or biological causes for criminal behaviour. One reason for this is that biological accounts of criminality do not obviously lead to suggestions about how criminality can be reduced. Additionally, there is a danger that individuals may be stigmatised – without ever having committed a crime – if they are found to have genetic or biological features supposed to be 'markers' for criminal tendencies.

Progress exercise

At AS Level you will have looked at different ways of conducting research and may well have learned about different ways of studying the brain. How would you investigate Mitchells' and Blair's suggestion that psychopaths have a dysfunctional amygdala? Which research design would you use? Which technique for studying the brain would be most appropriate?

EYSENCK'S PERSONALITY THEORY

Eysenck's theory of criminality suggests that criminal behaviour arises from particular personality traits. Although Eysenck's personality theory is usually considered to have more of a 'psychological' than a 'biological' flavour, it is included in this chapter because Eysenck suggested that personality traits are biological in origin. Originally, Eysenck proposed that most of the variations between people could be reduced to just two dimensions of personality, neuroticism (N) and extraversion (E). These should not be thought of as types of people but rather as dimensions along which people can vary. A person with high N is prone to unstable moods, depression and anxiety whereas a person low in N tends to be emotionally stable. The E dimension relates to the amount of stimulation a person requires from their environment. Someone high in E requires a great deal of external stimulation whilst a person low in E requires very little. Eysenck devised simple **psychometric tests** (e.g. the Eysenck Personality Questionnaire or EPQ) to measure these traits and considered them to be normally distributed in the population. That is, the majority of people score neither very high nor very low.

Eysenck proposed that the E and N traits he described related to general properties of the human central nervous system. E relates to a person's overall level of cortical and autonomic arousal. The lower this is, the more stimulation the person requires from their environment. Hence, extraverts require excitement because their CNS and ANS are chronically under-stimulated. The N dimension relates to the stability of a person's CNS. A high N score denotes an individual whose nervous system reacts very strongly to aversive stimuli. Due to their high anxiety levels, Eysenck believed people with high N score to be difficult to condition. That is, it is more difficult for them to learn socially appropriate behaviours (e.g. not behaving aggressively) through the normal means of reinforcement and punishment.

Eysenck originally suggested that criminal behaviours were more likely in people with high E and high N scores. The combination of these two traits would result in a person who constantly sought excitement and stimulation (because of their high E) but who did not learn from their mistakes or punishments (due to high N). Thus the normal processes of socialisation (see above) would fail to work properly on such an individual, resulting in a high probability of criminal behaviour. Eysenck later suggested the existence of a third personality dimension, psychoticism (P). High P scores characterise people who are cold, uncaring, solitary and aggressive. As with E and N, Eysenck believed that P is largely genetic and that individuals with extreme P scores are highly likely to engage in criminal behaviour.

Evaluation of Eysenck's theory

Eysenck's (1964) personality theory of criminality generates predictions that are relatively easy to test. If it is true that high E, N and P lead to criminal behaviour then we would expect to find generally higher E, N and P scores in populations of offenders. Although Eysenck himself claimed impressive support for his theory, other researchers have suggested that matters are not so clear. Farrington et al. (1982) reviewed a number of studies and concluded that officially defined offenders (e.g. prisoners) generally scored higher than controls on P and N but not E. In contrast, a number of studies which have correlated E with self-report measures of delinquency have found that they do appear to be related (e.g. Rushton and Christjohn 1981). Hollin (1989) summarises a number of studies and concludes that offender groups consistently score higher than controls on measures of P and N. However, the relationship between offending and E is inconsistent, with some studies showing offenders to have higher E than controls, some lower and some about the same.

Eysenck's theory has stimulated a great deal of research and there is some support for his claims. However, a number of important criticisms have been made of it. First, there is the inconsistency of the findings relating to E scores amongst offenders. One possibility is that the E scale actually measures two different things, impulsiveness and sociability. There is some evidence that offender groups score higher than controls on impulsiveness but not sociability. Second, some researchers have taken issue with Eysenck's concept of P, because it is unclear exactly what it is measuring. It appears to be related to psychopathic tendencies but not in a consistent way (Blackburn 1993). Third, some researchers have criticised Eysenck's notion of personality as a set of traits that are consistent across situations. Mischel (1968), for example, suggests that apparent consistencies in the way people behave can be explained by the fact that people are usually observed in similar situations. If this is accepted it becomes unnecessary to propose that personality traits as such exist. Overall, however, it can be concluded that Eysenck's theory has been useful in describing how certain measurable tendencies might increase the likelihood of a person becoming involved in criminal activities. As such it is of potentially considerable use in identifying risk factors for criminality. However, on its own it does not constitute a complete theory of criminal behaviour.

Chapter summary

Early attempts to explain criminality in terms of a single inherited characteristic have not been well supported by research. However, there is some evidence that criminal tendencies are inherited. It is currently unknown exactly how genes influence criminal behaviour but it is likely that genetics and environment interact in complex ways. Some criminal behaviour appears to have a neurological component and there is increasing evidence that psychopathy originates within amygdala dysfunction. Eysenck's personality theory, whilst not explaining criminal behaviour, goes some way to showing how inherited characteristics might lead to criminal behaviour in certain contexts. In general, it is probably wrong to talk about genetic and biological causes of criminal behaviour but it is likely that these factors can contribute to criminality in some ways.

Further reading

P.B. Ainsworth (2000) *Psychology and Crime: Myths and Reality*. Harlow: Pearson Education. Chapter 4 contains a very useful overview of constitutional and genetic research into criminality.

R. Blackburn (1993) *The Psychology of Criminal Conduct*. Chichester: Wiley. Chapter 6 contains a technical but extremely thorough examination of the genetic and biological correlates of offending.

4

Psychologically oriented explanations of criminal behaviour

◪ Psychoanalytical theories of crime
◇ Learning theories of crime
◪ Cognitive theories of crime
◢ Social theories of crime

The previous chapter examined criminality from a biological perspective. By contrast, this chapter looks at a range of theories of criminality originating in psychological perspectives. A huge variety of factors have been related to criminal behaviour. A small number of these are discussed here including unconscious motivations (the psychoanalytical approach), learning experiences (e.g. social learning theory), cognitive processes (e.g. moral reasoning) and social factors (e.g. self-fulfilling prophecies). The range of theories included here is by no means exhaustive but gives some indication of the variety of possible ways of understanding crime from a psychological point of view.

PSYCHOANALYTICAL THEORIES OF CRIME

Psychoanalytical approaches to crime stress the importance of irrational, unconscious motivations in criminal behaviour. A number of psychoanalytical thinkers have turned their attention to crime, seeing

Progress exercise

At AS Level you will have studied a variety of approaches to psychology, such as the psychodynamic, cognitive and behavioural approaches. Identify two approaches you have studied and suggest how each of them would attempt to explain criminal behaviour. Make a note of the differences and similarities between the two approaches.

it as one possible manifestation of unconscious pathological processes. There is no general psychoanalytical theory of crime but many psychoanalytical accounts have features in common that will be examined here. Bowlby's theory of the role of maternal deprivation in delinquency also has its roots in the psychoanalytical approach and will be discussed in this section.

Psychoanalytical conceptions of crime

Within the psychoanalytical framework, the personality is supposed to have three components. At the root of the psyche is the id, which generates self-serving and pleasure-seeking impulses. If manifested, these would result in highly antisocial behaviour. The pleasure-oriented demands of the id are redirected by the ego, whose primary orientation is towards reality. The ego, in turn, is guided by the superego, which embodies the moral rules that a person acquires during socialisation within the family. If the ego acts contrary to the superego's moral rules it is punished with guilt and anxiety. In a well-adjusted person, the ego is able to act in a way that satisfies the id's demands for gratification but in a way that is morally acceptable to the superego.

It follows from this that tendencies to behave antisocially are, from a psychoanalytical viewpoint, the result of an inadequate or dysfunctional superego which, in turn, results from an abnormal relationship with the parents during childhood. Criminal behaviour can be the result of a superego which is over-harsh, weak or deviant (Blackburn 1993). If the superego is excessively harsh and punitive, the person may be prone to engage in criminal behaviour (e.g. 'compulsive' stealing) in order to be punished for it. Here, the desire to be punished is related to guilt over unconscious infantile desires. Conversely, a person with a weak superego would feel less, if any, guilt or anxiety over contemplated antisocial acts. Since it is this anxiety and guilt which keeps most people 'on the straight and narrow' the person would have few inhibitions against acting on selfish and aggressive impulses from the id. In the psychoanalytical literature, this state of affairs has chiefly been invoked to explain the characteristics of the psychopath. The third possibility, that of a deviant superego, is exemplified by a state of affairs in which a young boy has a good relationship with a criminal father. In internalising his father's values in the usual course of development he would, incidentally, internalise his father's criminal attributes (Blackburn 1993). Consequently, his superego would simply not react negatively to contemplated criminal acts.

Evaluation of psychoanalytical research into crime

There is a tendency to dismiss psychoanalytically derived theories out of hand on the grounds that they are 'unscientific'. This may not be wholly fair. Blackburn (1993) points out that psychoanalytical theories are characterised by a number of assumptions: first, that socialisation depends on childhood experiences and, second, that poor quality parent-child interaction is related to later delinquent tendencies. These two assumptions are shared by a number of theories besides psychoanalysis. The third assumption, that criminal tendencies are a manifestation of unconscious conflict, is the most crucial to psychoanalysis and, unfortunately, the most difficult to gather direct evidence for. However, Hollin (1989) observes that researchers within this framework have identified a number of important variables relating to delinquent behaviour in adolescence. Therefore, psychoanalytical research has provided useful pointers to later theorists of crime. It should be stressed, however, that the relationship between family variables and criminality can be explained in a number of ways (e.g. through social learning) and that it is relatively rare now for researchers to rely solely on psychoanalytical theories in explaining criminal behaviour.

Bowlby: maternal deprivation and delinquency

One of the best-known psychoanalytically derived theories of delinquency was put forward by John Bowlby (1951). Bowlby's **maternal deprivation theory**, although originating within psychoanalysis, also contains elements of ethology and evolutionary theory. Essentially, Bowlby proposed that a child requires a close and continuous relationship with its primary caregiver up to the age of about 5. If this attachment relationship is disrupted then a consequence can be an inability in the child to form meaningful relationships with other people. In some individuals, this 'affectionless' character might lead to delinquent behaviour. Bowlby's theory was based on evidence derived from studying juvenile delinquents referred to a child guidance clinic. He compared forty-four juvenile thieves to a matched group of non-delinquents. He found that 39 per cent of the delinquent group had experienced significant disruption of their maternal attachments before the age of 5, compared to only 5 per cent of the non-delinquent group.

Evaluation of Bowlby's theory

Although a great number of studies support the view that disturbance within the family is related to delinquency, it is no longer widely accepted that there is a causal link between maternal deprivation and criminal tendencies. Later research (e.g. Rutter 1971) did not produce results as clear-cut as Bowlby's original study, which has been criticised on a number of counts including the unrepresentative nature of his sample and his poor control group matching (Hollin 1989). Rutter concludes that there is little evidence to suggest that disruption of the attachment relationship is causally related to delinquency. One major problem is that Bowlby did not adequately distinguish between the disruption of attachments (an attachment forms but is then discontinued), the privation of attachment (an attachment never forms) and the distortion of attachments (they are affected by adverse circumstances such as parental conflict). It is possible that distortion or privation, but not deprivation *per se*, will result in deviant behaviour later in life (Marshall 1983). Generally, though, Bowlby overestimated the extent to which early experiences have a permanent impact on later development (Ainsworth 2000).

LEARNING THEORIES OF CRIME

The learning approach to psychology views crime as a set of behaviours learned in the same way as any other. This approach to criminality stresses the role of the family and peer group as sources of criminal behaviour and the role of reinforcement and punishment in determining whether a person embarks upon a criminal career. A particularly important theory from this perspective is Sutherland's (1939) differential association theory of crime. This section will also examine the social learning theory and the view that exposure to violent media is a factor in aggressive tendencies.

Differential association theory

Sutherland's basic suggestion is that criminal behaviour is learned through exposure to criminal norms. This happens within the family and peer group. Criminality arises from two factors, learned attitudes and imitation of specific acts. In Sutherland's view, criminal behaviour is an expression of needs and values, for example, the need for money. However, the need for money cannot be used to explain criminal behaviours: these are learned. When a person is socialised within a group (e.g. the family; peer groups) they will be exposed to values and attitudes towards the law. Some of these values and attitudes will be favourable, some unfavourable. If a person comes to acquire more favourable attitudes towards crime than unfavourable ones, then they may become a criminal. They may also acquire from their social groups specific techniques for breaking the law. It is important to realise that, in Sutherland's view, a person does not necessarily learn deviant attitudes from other criminals. For example, it is entirely possible for parents who are law abiding to express disapproval of the law or the police. Additionally, a person does not necessarily learn favourable attitudes towards all forms of crime: a person who thinks that burglary is wrong may nonetheless feel that it is acceptable to falsify a tax return (Hollin 1989).

Evaluation of differential association theory

The differential association theory states that people who become criminals will have been socialised within groups with at least some pro-criminal norms. It follows that there should be evidence of pro-criminal norms (and probably criminal activity) within the families and/or the peer groups of criminals. There is some evidence to support this hypothesis. As was discussed in Chapter 3, in the context of genetic contributions to crime, people with criminal parents run a higher risk of becoming criminals themselves. It also seems that juvenile delinquents are more likely than non-delinquents to report having friends who also engage in antisocial activities (Matthews 1968). However, there are some problems with this evidence. First, Blackburn (1993) found that this pattern applies mainly to vandalism and petty theft rather than more serious offences. Second, the evidence is correlational and it is difficult to say what the direction of causality is. It is possible that, rather than becoming delinquent through association with other delinquents, people with delinquent tendencies select delinquent friends.

A number of additional problems are associated with the differential association theory. Some of the concepts within the theory are rather vaguely defined. It is difficult to see, for example, how the number of pro-criminal values a person has could be directly measured. Additionally, the theory fails to specify exactly the extent to which pro-criminal values must outnumber anti-criminal ones for the individual to become a criminal. The theory also fails to account for individual differences in criminality, that is, why some people exposed to 'criminogenic' influences become criminals whilst others exposed to the same influences do not. Blackburn (1993) states that, whist the differential association theory explains the acquisition of criminal *tendencies* it does not account for the performance and maintenance of criminal behaviours. That is, you can learn *how* to be a criminal from others, but this does not necessarily mean that you will commit crimes.

Social learning theory

An alternative approach to the acquisition of criminal behaviour is the **social learning theory** (SLT). This approach, chiefly associated with the work of Albert Bandura, suggests that behaviours of any sort may be learned by observing others. Those individuals who are observed are known as **models**. Whether or not a person will be selected as a model depends on a range of variables including their status. Whether or not a model's behaviour will be imitated depends chiefly on the consequences of their actions: if they are seen to be reinforced for their behaviour then the observer is more likely to imitate them. Conversely, if the model is seen to be punished the observer is less likely to imitate their behaviour (these processes are called vicarious reinforcement and punishment). SLT is a general approach to psychology and regards criminal behaviour as qualitatively no different from any other kind, stating that it is learned through the processes of observation, imitation and vicarious reinforcement and punishment. SLT shares many ideas with differential association theory. However, as a theory it tends to avoid the more nebulously defined concepts such as 'criminal norms'.

Evaluation of social learning theory

The most obvious way in which social learning theory has contributed to the understanding of criminal behaviour is in its application to the acquisition of aggressive responses. Bandura et al. (1963) demonstrated in a classic study that young children could acquire aggressive behaviours through the observation of an adult model. A group of 4 and 5 year olds observed an adult behaving aggressively (both verbally and physically) towards an inflatable toy known as a bobo doll. Some of the children observed the model being reinforced for this by being praised by another adult. A second group observed the model being punished (told off). A control group observed the aggressive behaviour being neither reinforced nor punished. When later given an opportunity to play with the bobo doll the children who had observed the aggressive model being reinforced were seen to imitate many of the verbal and physical behaviours exhibited by the adult. Imitation of the model was also observed in the control group. Those children who had seen the model punished were comparatively much less likely to behave aggressively towards the bobo doll. It is important to note that all the children, including those who saw the model punished, had *learned* the model's aggressive behaviour. When later offered reinforcement for behaving aggressively towards the doll they produced just as many aggressive acts as the group who had initially seen the model reinforced. In other words, all the children acquired, through observing the model, competence in aggressive behaviours. Whether or not they performed these behaviours depended on the consequences they observed for the model. There is, therefore, abundant evidence from studies such as Bandura et al. (1963) to show that children are capable of learning by observation.

One of the major strengths of SLT is that it stresses the uniqueness of the individual and concedes that different people may commit the same crimes for different reasons. This is because each individual's motivations and expectations are based on their unique learning experiences. However, SLT has come under criticism on a number of grounds. First, SLT has a tendency to underplay the role of cognitive factors, such as decision making, in criminal behaviour. Most social learning theorists now recognise that this is a serious drawback of the theory in its original form and have responded by modifying SLT to take more account of cognitive factors (e.g. Bandura's 1986 social cognitive approach). A second criticism of SLT is that it is based largely on laboratory studies. Laboratory studies suffer from a number of problems, such as their artificiality, which mean that it can be unwise to generalise from them. According to Blackburn (1993) social learning theorists have largely neglected naturalistic research and as a result the validity of many of their findings must be called into question. A final problem with SLT is that it is **determinist**. In other words, SLT states that an individual's behaviour is completely determined by their learning experiences and does not acknowledge the possibility of freedom of choice. Some researchers object to this idea on philosophical grounds. It must be stated, however, that the issue of whether people have free will is an extremely complex one that, strictly speaking, is impossible to resolve once and for all (see Gross 1991 for an overview). However, it is worth noting that, in this respect, many psychological approaches to criminality are in direct conflict with legal conceptions of crime. Legal definitions of crime implicitly acknowledge that the individual has freedom of choice and is therefore responsible for their actions. By contrast, psychological explanations of criminality tend to stress the role of factors outside the individual's control.

The media-aggression hypothesis

Early studies such as Bandura et al. (1963) highlighted the possibility that children could learn to behave in aggressive ways through observing aggression in the media. Of the available media, television and cinema were singled out for special attention although, more recently, violent video games have been subject to scrutiny. In the years since Bandura's early work a great number of studies have been conducted into the possible link between violent media and aggressive behaviour in society.

Laboratory research

Much early work was conducted in the laboratory. For example, Berkowitz (1969) showed participants either violent or non-violent films. When later given the opportunity to aggress against another person by giving electric shocks, those who had watched the violent film gave more shocks. Findings like this appear to offer clear-cut evidence for the influence of the media on aggressive behaviour until it is considered that they were obtained under highly artificial conditions. Research that is more naturalistic less obviously supports the media-aggression hypothesis although there are a few noteworthy findings. Williams (1986) studied a small community in Canada where television had recently been introduced for the first time. Observational, teacher and peer ratings of children's aggression were compared with similar measures taken from two other communities. In one of these, there was a single television channel operating and in the other, there were several. Williams reports that over a two-year period aggression in the community where television had just been introduced rose steadily whilst in those where television was already available there was no such rise. This appears to support the hypothesis that aggressive media content and aggressive behaviour are linked.

Correlation studies

An alternative way of studying the effects of the media is through correlation studies. In a typical study of this type, ratings of children's aggressiveness are compared with their television preferences in order to see if violent viewing and aggressive behaviour are linked. Results from such studies are mixed. Belson (1978) conducted a retrospective study in which teenage boys were questioned about their viewing habits and their tendencies to behave aggressively. The data suggested that those who watched a great deal of violent programming content were more likely to use violence in their everyday lives.

There are, however, a number of problems with this research approach. First, the data were gathered retrospectively and thus may not accurately reflect actual viewing or behaviour. Second, the link between the two variables is correlational. It is not possible to conclude that watching violent programmes made the participants more aggressive. It could be that people with a tendency to behave more aggressively seek out programmes that are more violent. Alternatively, it may be that some third variable influences both viewing preferences and aggressive tendencies. Milarsky et al. (1982) attempted to address these issues in a study in which 3,200 schoolchildren of various ages were interviewed a number of times about their viewing habits and their verbally and physically aggressive behaviour. In this study, only small associations were found between exposure to violent media and actual aggressive behaviour. Compared to other variables, such as family background, television appeared to have a minor effect on how aggressively the participants behaved.

Evaluation of the media-aggression hypothesis

The evidence regarding the effect of violent media on aggressive behaviour is far from clear and it would be unwise to state unequivocally that the two are directly linked. If media violence does lead to aggressive behaviour, its influence is likely to be small. However, one possibility that should be considered is that certain individuals are particularly vulnerable to the effects of violent media. As such they may be prone to 'acting out' the violence they have observed on screen (sometimes referred to as **copycat crimes**). Although this remains a possibility there is currently no way of identifying such individuals and it is not clear what might be done about them if they could be identified. Additionally, Howitt (1998) points out that much of the evidence for copycat crimes is flawed and often so-called copycat crimes have very little to do with the media.

Progress exercise

Is it a good idea to try to reduce the amount of violence shown in television programmes? Would this reduce violence in society?

COGNITIVE THEORIES OF CRIME

As discussed above, one of the major drawbacks of social learning theory is the extent to which it ignores the role of cognition, or thinking. Alternative theories give cognition a central role in criminal behaviour. Of the many theories that have been put forward, three will be considered in this section. These are Yochelson and Samenow's (1976) theory of the 'criminal personality', Kohlberg's (1976) theory of moral development and the rational choice theory of crime put forward by Cornish and Clark (1987).

Yochelson and Samenow's 'criminal personality'

Yochelson and Samenow (1976) propose that criminality is an attribute of personality. However, they do not follow Eysenck in ascribing personality to innate properties of the nervous system. Rather, they take a cognitive view that emphasises the role of biases and errors in thinking in criminal behaviour. They suggest that personality develops over the life-span and is heavily influenced by parent-child interaction in childhood. Yochelson and Samenow believe that all behaviour is the result of a rational thinking process. Criminals, due to the errors and biases in their thinking, arrive at behavioural strategies that are unacceptable to the majority of people. Based on interviews with 240 male offenders drawn from a variety of settings including community clinics and psychiatric hospitals, Yochelson and Samenow propose that the criminal personality features forty 'thinking errors' (that is, habitual biases and distortions in decision making) which can be grouped into three types. Some of these are outlined in Table 4.1.

Evaluation of Yochelson and Samenow's theory

Yochelson and Samenow deny that criminals are ever impulsive since fantasies and premeditation will have preceded any crime a person commits. As such, their theory coincides with the **rational choice theory** of crime, which has recently been gaining in popularity (see below). However, their theory suffers from a number of problems. First, Yochelson and Samenow appear not to have compared their criminal sample with a non-criminal control group. They have therefore not established that their 'criminal' thinking errors do not occur in

Table 4.1 Thinking errors of Yochelson and Samenow's 'Criminal Personality'

	Character traits	Automatic errors of thinking	Errors associated with criminal acts
Types of error	• Feelings of worthlessness • Need for power and control • Perfectionism • Lying	• Poor decision making • Lack of trust • Failure to assume obligations	• Fantasies of antisocial behaviour • Super-optimism

the non-criminal population. Second, their sample of criminals is unrepresentative of offenders generally. Third, their 'thinking errors' are not based on any mainstream theory of decision making (e.g. rational choice theory, see below) although Wulach (1988) points out that many of them appear to resemble psychoanalytical defence mechanisms. Wulach adds that the thinking patterns described by Yochelson and Samenow resemble a number of personality disorders described in *DSM-III-R* (the manual of psychological disorders) and therefore do not constitute a unique personality type. To conclude, Yochelson and Samenow's research should be applauded for the cognitive approach it takes to criminal behaviour. However, its unsystematic nature means that it is of limited value in understanding criminality.

Moral development and crime

Kohlberg's (1976) theory of moral development is not a theory of crime as such. However, since it is concerned with how people's moral thinking develops it is of potential relevance to understanding criminal behaviour. Kohlberg was chiefly concerned with the cognitive processes underlying moral judgements. Following the work of Piaget (1959), Kohlberg suggested that, in line with more general intellectual development, moral reasoning advances with increasing age. Kohlberg investigated moral reasoning in children and adults using a number of moral dilemmas. In each of these, the participant is given a moral dilemma in the form of a short scenario and asked what would be the correct course of action to take. The most famous such dilemma concerns a man whose wife is dying but who cannot afford the medicine that might save her. The participant is asked whether the man should break into a pharmacy and steal the medicine. Kohlberg was not so much interested in whether the participant answered yes or no but wished to examine the reasoning behind their decision. From the kinds of reasons that people gave, he distinguished between three distinct levels of moral reasoning. Each level contains two stages, giving six stages in all. Table 4.2 outlines the types of moral reasoning evident at each stage.

Evaluation of Kohlberg's theory

Based on Kohlberg's theory it seems reasonable to suggest, since crime often represents a choice of immoral action, that criminals will show a generally lower level of moral reasoning than will non-criminals. However, two important points should be remembered. First, it was not Kohlberg's intention to produce a theory of crime. Second, Kohlberg's theory concerns moral *reasoning*, not moral *behaviour*. Although it is an assumption of the theory that moral reasoning motivates moral action, it is obvious that anyone can have high moral standards that they fail to live up to. Bearing these points in mind, there is some evidence that appears to support the idea that delinquents show a lower level of moral reasoning than do non-delinquents. Arbuthnot et al. (1987) reviewed fifteen studies and found that in all but three, significantly more delinquents than non-delinquents were functioning at level 2 than level 3. Thornton (1987) also reports a study that found a correlation between adolescents' level of moral reasoning and teacher ratings of antisocial behaviour. Blackburn (1993) suggests that delinquents may show poor moral development because of a lack of role-playing opportunities in childhood, through which their moral reasoning might have been extended.

Although research like this supports the idea of a link between poor moral development and delinquency a number of points need to be stressed. First, the relationship only seems to exist for officially defined

Table 4.2 **Levels and stages of moral development in Kohlberg's theory**

Level	Stage	Description
Pre-conventional Rules and social expectations are external to the individual.	Obedience and punishment orientation	'Right' and 'wrong' are determined by what is punished and what is not.
	Instrumental purpose and exchange	'Right' and 'wrong' are determined by what brings rewards, rather than the avoidance of punishment.
Conventional The individual has internalised the rules and expectations of others.	Interpersonal accord and conformity	'Right' is defined in terms of what pleases others.
	Social accord and system maintenance	'Right' is defined in terms of conformity and respect for authority.
Post-conventional The individual adopts universal moral principles and distinguishes their rules from the rules and expectations of others.	Social contract, utility and moral rights	'Right' and 'wrong' are determined by values and opinions. Individual rights can be more important than laws.

Universal ethical principles	'Right' and 'wrong' are based on ethical principles adopted by the person that are essentially separate from the mores of society although the two may coincide.

delinquents. The same relationship is not found between moral development and self-reports of offending. Second, the relationship is stronger for some types of offenders and offences than others. For example, Thornton and Reid (1982) found that those convicted of crimes carried out for material gain (such as robbery and theft) were more likely to show pre-conventional moral reasoning than those convicted of impulsive crimes like assault. This is not surprising given that the former types of crime involve planning and, hence, reasoning whereas the latter type does not. Finally, Blackburn (1993) notes that it is currently unknown how moral reasoning interacts with personality and situational factors in influencing moral behaviour. In conclusion, whilst there is a relationship between moral reasoning and delinquency, Kohlberg's theory on its own is not enough to explain criminal behaviour and should be considered as complementary to other explanations of offending.

Rational choice theory

As discussed above, the chief contribution of Yochelson and Samenow's research was to suggest that criminal behaviour is the outcome of a reasoned decision-making process. This idea is central to the **rational choice theory** of crime (RCT) put forward by Cornish and Clark (1987). RCT is based on a number of assumptions. The most important of these is that criminals seek to benefit from the crimes they commit. Their decision to commit a crime is based on a consideration of whether the benefits (e.g. material gain) outweigh the potential costs (e.g. effort, getting caught). The decision-making process is not completely logical but is constrained by a number of factors including the time available, the information possessed by the offender and factors such as the offender's cognitive ability. However, RCT essentially states that offenders *choose* specific crimes for specific reasons and in order to understand why a given offender commits a particular crime we need to understand the factors that have influenced their decision-making process.

Evaluation of rational choice theory

A number of studies have supported the idea that the decision to commit certain types of crime is the outcome of a rational process. Rettig (1966) gave students a hypothetical scenario describing an opportunity to commit a crime. He gave the students different relevant information about the crime (e.g. likely benefits, risk of detection, likely degree of punishment) and found that the degree of punishment exerted the most influence on the students' decision to commit the crime. Feldman (1977) carried out a similar study on younger participants and found that the vast majority of decisions to commit the crime were rational (i.e. if potential rewards were high and costs low then the crime was worth carrying out). However, it must be stressed that these experiments were simulations using students and the results may not apply to real offenders. However, Bennett and Wright (1984) interviewed a number of convicted burglars about their decisions to break into particular properties and found results consistent with RCT. The burglars' reasons could be grouped into three major factors: risk (e.g. chance of being seen or caught), reward (potential material gain) and ease of entry (how difficult the property would be to break into). Of these factors, risk was the most important in determining whether or not they would carry out a particular crime.

Although this research generally supports RCT, there are a number of points that must be stressed. First, Bennett and Wright's research involved convicted (i.e. unsuccessful) burglars and it may be that the reasoning processes of more successful criminals are different. Second, not all crimes are planned and rationally thought out. Many violent crimes, for example, appear to be impulsive responses to the immediate situation. For this reason, RCT cannot really be regarded as a theory of crime but rather an explanation of how some individuals approach certain types of crime. Cornish and Clark (1987) admit as much and suggest that their approach be regarded as a perspective on crime from which specific theories of offending can be developed. In this respect, RCT has proven a useful tool for developing explanations for a range of crimes including shoplifting, robbery and drug use (Hollin 1989).

SOCIAL THEORIES OF CRIME

Social theories of crime share the assumption that criminal tendencies and behaviour are acquired from the social environment, that is, the people by whom the offender is socialised and those with whom they come into contact. As such, the differential association theory and the social learning theory (both discussed above) qualify as social theories as much as they do learning theories and could equally have been included in this section. Bearing this in mind, only one major theory – labelling theory – will be discussed here although some consideration will be given to a related process known as **self-fulfilling prophecy**.

Labelling theory

Labelling theory is based on the idea that society's reaction to deviance (the violation of norms) has consequences for the future behaviour of the deviant person. It has been applied to a range of phenomena including mental health but as it applies to criminality, it works in the following way. Society defines certain acts (e.g. stealing) as criminal. The person who commits such acts is labelled by society as 'a criminal'. Having been labelled in this way, the person is treated by society in a way that is consistent with the 'criminal' label. For example, they are stigmatised and subject to the sanctions of the judicial system (fines, imprisonment and so on). Because the person is treated in this way they come to adopt the label 'criminal' as part of their self-image and this affects their future behaviour. In short, a person adopts a criminal career as a consequence of being labelled a criminal.

Evaluation of labelling theory

The central assumption of labelling theory is that the label applied to the person is incorporated into the person's self-concept. If this is true then we might expect to find that the self-concepts of delinquents would contain more 'deviant' elements than those of non-offenders. Some research supports this view. For example, Ageton and Elliot (1974) examined the self-concept of a number of adolescent boys who had never come into contact with the police. Those who subsequently were arrested tended to adopt delinquent self-descriptions whilst the self-concepts of boys who were not labelled by the authorities remained the same. However, this has not been a consistent finding and many studies have shown that a delinquent self-concept tends to be present before any contact with the authorities (Gibbs 1974). Other studies have shown that delinquent labelling does not affect all people in the same way, and has a greater effect on youths with a higher socio-economic status (Klein 1986). Blackburn (1993) suggests that labelling theory over-simplifies the relationship between attitudes, self-concept and behaviour. He concludes that evidence in favour of the theory is weak but concedes that it may have some utility in understanding delinquency, especially in the light of studies which have confirmed self-fulfilling prophecies in other contexts (e.g. education).

Self-fulfilling prophecy

Labelling theory is derived chiefly from sociology but is paralleled by the social-psychological idea of **self-fulfilling prophecy**. This is a prediction that comes true because it has been made. For example, a teacher who believes that a pupil is unintelligent may devote less time and attention to him, mark his work more harshly and so on. This might result in the pupil becoming demotivated, ceasing to apply him-self and eventually performing very poorly, confirming the prediction originally made by the teacher. Some research into the role of self-fulfilling prophecies with offenders has been carried out. Jahoda (1954) reports that amongst the Ashanti people of Western Africa there is a practice of naming boys according to the day on which they are born. The day of birth is thought to determine the boy's temperament, so, for example, boys born on a Monday are believed to be placid, whereas those born on a Wednesday are supposed to be aggressive. Police records apparently showed a high number of arrests for boys born on a Wednesday compared with a very low number for those born on a Monday. Jahoda concludes that the boys' names influenced how they were treated by others, resulting in different patterns of behaviour. Meichenbaum et al. (1969) conducted a study using female juvenile delinquents. Six were selected from a class of fourteen and their teachers were told that they were 'late developers' with strong academic potential. Observations showed that the teachers began to behave differently towards them and the girls subsequently performed better than matched controls in examinations. However, beyond a few isolated studies, little research has concentrated directly on the role of self-fulfilling prophecy in causing criminal behaviour. The main reason for this is that it would be highly unethical to deliberately label people as criminals in order to test the theory.

How could the ideas of labelling and self-fulfilling prophecy be used to explain Sheldon's finding that criminality and bodily build appear to be linked?

Progress exercise

Chapter summary

Many psychological theories of offending share some common ground. In particular, they tend to emphasise the role of the environment in the learning of criminal tendencies and behaviours. Psychodynamic approaches to crime stress the role of unconscious motivations in criminal behaviour. Although such theories have provided useful pointers to other researchers, they have, in themselves, little explanatory value. Learning theories are based around the acquisition of criminal values and behaviours from the family and peer group. It is a general criticism of learning theories that they tend to over-simplify criminal behaviour, particularly in their relative neglect of cognitive factors in offending. Cognitive approaches to understanding criminality include Yochelson and Samenow's theory of the criminal personality. Although this emphasises the role of thinking biases and errors in criminal behaviour it was based on unsystematic research and has little explanatory value. Kohlberg's theory of moral development can make some contribution to our understanding of criminal behaviour but this will always be limited by the fact that criminality was not Kohlberg's primary focus. Recently, systematic cognitive theories like rational choice theory have arisen although it should be stressed that this approach applies only to certain types of crime and offender. Given the variation in the types of possible offence and the types of people committing them it is unlikely that there will ever be a single explanation for all forms of criminal behaviour.

Further reading

P. B. Ainsworth (2000) *Psychology and Crime: Myths and Reality*. Harlow: Pearson Education. Chapter 4 contains good coverage of a range of psychological theories of crime.

The majority of general and social psychology textbooks contain fairly comprehensive coverage of the media aggression debate.

The police and crime

◤ Policing
◇ Interviewing
◤ Negotiation

POLICING

In the UK and most other countries, the police serve a wide range of functions. These primarily entail enforcing the criminal law and investigating criminal offences but include a variety of other tasks including giving advice on crime prevention, controlling crowds and regulating traffic (Bayley 1979). This chapter will examine a number of aspects of policing. First, the question will be discussed of whether there is a distinct type of person who becomes a police officer. Next, some consideration will be given to how the police determine who is a suspect in a crime and how different variables affect the way suspects are processed. There follows a discussion of some of the interview techniques employed by the police including techniques that enhance witness recall and the issues surrounding false confessions. Finally, there is an examination of the negotiation techniques that can be employed, for example, in hostage situations.

The police personality

A number of researchers have investigated the police as people and have produced some evidence suggesting that police officers tend to have certain personality characteristics. Fenster et al. (1973) compared a sample of US police officers with civilians and found that they were, on average, less dogmatic and neurotic and had slightly higher IQ scores. In the UK, Gudjonsson and Adlam (1983) compared police officers with controls using the Eysenck Personality Questionnaire (see Chapter 3 for an overview of Eysenck's personality theory). They found that the police scored higher on measures of extraversion (E) but lower on measures of psychoticism (P). This indicates that police tend to be outgoing and relatively lacking in coldness and aggressiveness. Further personality testing found that officers tended to have lower scores on measures of empathy. This does not necessarily indicate that police officers are unfeeling people but rather that they tend not to become emotionally involved in their work. Gudjonsson and Adlam suggest that this may reflect a strategy for coping with the more unpleasant aspects of police work.

An unresolved debate concerns whether these small differences between police officers and civilians represent socialisation or disposition. The dispositional approach suggests that individuals with certain personality characteristics are drawn towards police work whereas the socialisation approach would claim that individuals are 'moulded' by police work to produce the characteristics of the 'police personality'. Some research apparently supports the dispositional view. For example, Austin et al. (1987) carried out a longitudinal study looking at people who had left the force. They found that their personality remained relatively stable. On the other hand, Adlam (1981) found evidence that some characteristics, such as cynicism, increased with the amount of time spent on the force. This would seem to support the socialisation approach. Ultimately, it is likely that both approaches are correct to some extent. Police work will initially be more attractive to people with certain personality characteristics. Those who are unsuited to police work may leave the force. At the same time, the experience of police work and immersion in police culture will alter those who remain. Unfortunately, there has been a lack of detailed longitudinal studies which might help to resolve this issue (Hollin 1989).

Determining and processing suspects

Research into the way the police determine and process suspects concentrates firstly on who the police are likely to arrest and secondly on how they are likely to deal with the arrestee.

Progress exercise

It is often claimed that the police are biased in the way they determine and process suspects. Before reading the following section, make a list of the types of people you think police officers are most likely to be biased against. Suggest why they may be targeted. Then, compare your answers with the research findings in this section.

Factors influencing arrest

Only a minority of incidents to which the police are called result in an arrest. Whether or not a person is arrested depends chiefly on factors such as the seriousness of the offence and how insistent the complainant (if any) is. However, there is some evidence suggesting that the characteristics and behaviour of the suspect also influence their chance of being arrested. Black and Reiss (1970) observed 281 incidents involving juveniles. They found that 15 per cent of incidents led to an arrest. The most important factor in determining arrest was the seriousness of the offence. However, they also found that 21 per cent of black suspects were arrested compared to only 8 per cent of white suspects. This might appear to indicate a racial bias on the part of the police. However Black and Reiss found that the greater proportion of black suspects arrested was mainly a consequence of greater seriousness of offence amongst black youths and greater insistence on the part of complainants, the majority of whom were black themselves.

Other studies, however, have found evidence of racial bias in the arrest of suspects. Piliavin and Briar (1964) found that black youths were more likely to be stopped by the police. Additionally, Smith and Visher (1982) found that black suspects were more likely to be arrested even when other variables, such as offence seriousness, were controlled. Gibbens and Krohn (1986) found that police surveillance (e.g. patrols) tended to be concentrated in areas populated by ethnic minorities. Feldman (1993) suggests that this might explain Belson's (1975) finding that poorly educated lower SES juveniles were more likely than their more middle-class counterparts to be arrested. There has been no research that has directly attempted to establish this. Huizinga and Elliot (1987) analysed data from New York State and found that there were no differences between blacks and whites for either delinquent behaviour or high frequency offending. However, they found that black people were seven times more likely to be arrested for minor offences. For more serious offences, black people were twice as likely as white to be arrested.

Whilst these data support the notion of a racial bias in policing, several important points must be borne in mind. First, most of the data cited here were gathered in the US and matters may be different in the UK. Second, these studies are rather dated. Increasing efforts have been made in both the UK and the US to improve relations between ethnic minorities and the police, which may have affected the relative likelihood of black and white people being arrested. Finally, it is very likely that racial bias varies between police forces and between officers on the same force. These considerations mean that it cannot be assumed that all police officers are biased against members of ethnic minorities.

Another variable that appears to influence a suspect's chance of being arrested is their behaviour towards the police. Lundman et al. (1978) found that antagonistic or overly deferential youths were more likely to be arrested. Werner et al. (1975) found that youths who were polite, co-operative, presented identification promptly and answered questions were less likely to be arrested. This research indicates that non-legal factors have an influence on police decisions to make an arrest. However, it should be noted that these factors are more relevant to minor offences and when an offence is serious, arrest is almost universal (Piliavin and Briar 1964).

Disposal following arrest

Once a suspect has been arrested, the police have a choice regarding their course of action. The suspect may be released with no action taken, or the offence may be dealt with informally. Official means of dealing with arrested suspects involve either giving a formal caution or charging them with the offence. Cautions are recorded in the official crime statistics but divert offenders from court. As such, they are a preferred way of dealing with minor offences. Blackburn (1993) notes an increase in the use of cautions by the British police since the 1960s, from 10 per cent of offences in 1960 to 28 per cent in 1988. The major determining factors in whether a caution is given are the seriousness of the offence and the offender's history. First offenders are most likely to receive a caution, as are those arrested for petty offences. However, non-legal factors also affect the decision to either charge or caution the offender. Younger offenders (10–13 years) are more likely to be cautioned than charged, as are girls. Some studies have also indicated that race is a relevant factor. For example, Landau (1981) found that black youths were more likely to be charged than cautioned but only for offences of burglary, violence and public disorder.

The studies discussed above indicate that the decision to arrest and charge a suspect is chiefly determined by the offence of which they are accused. However, the influence of non-legal factors such as race, gender and demeanour suggests that police decisions are affected, at least to some extent, by a stereotype of a delinquent type who is presumably black, male, 'disrespectful' and uncooperative. There is a danger that this may lead, in some areas, to a 'downward spiral' in which apparent heavy-handedness by police disinclines youths to be co-operative which, in turn, leads to a greater chance of arrest (Gibbens and Krohn 1986)

INTERVIEWING

The police interview people for the purpose of obtaining information which may help them solve a crime. According to Gudjonsson (1992), people interviewed by the police typically fall into four categories:

- Victims are the people against whom an offence has been committed.
- Witnesses are people who may be able to supply information about the offence or offender.
- Complainants are the people who report the crime to the police.
- Suspects are the people who the police believe may have committed the crime.

These categories are not mutually exclusive. For example, both victims and complainants may also be witnesses. As far as the police are concerned, the important distinction is between witnesses and suspects. A broad distinction can be made between interviews, in which the police attempt to obtain information from witnesses, and **interrogations**, the purpose of which is to obtain a confession from a suspect.

Interview techniques

The goal of an interview is to obtain information that is complete and accurate. This is important because a witness statement may be used as evidence in a court case and it must therefore be seen as trustworthy or 'reliable'. According to Gudjonsson (1992) the **standard interview procedure** has four stages, referred to as 'orientation', 'listening', 'questions and answers' and 'advice'. In the first stage, the purpose of the interview is stated and legal requirements are fulfilled, such as informing the interviewee of their rights. The interviewee is then invited to give a free recall account of events, with minimal questions from the police. In the 'questions and answers' stage, the interviewer asks specific questions based on the person's free recall account. The purpose of this is to reduce ambiguities, fill in gaps and obtain additional information. Finally, the statement is read through. Alterations can be made and the interviewee is informed of any further action (e.g. the police may want to interview them again).

As the goal of interviewing is to obtain complete and accurate information, a great deal of research has investigated the factors that increase or decrease the reliability of the information obtained. Some of these, including **cognitive interview** techniques, are discussed in Chapter 7 in the context of witness testimony. This section considers factors that relate more directly to the interview itself. Gudjonsson (1992) identifies a range of such factors including communication and deception.

Gorden (1975) describes a number of factors that either facilitate or inhibit effective communication. Some of these are summarised in Table 5.1. In Gorden's view, an interviewer should always attempt to maximise facilitators and minimise inhibitors.

Gudjonsson (1992) points out that an important factor neglected by Gorden is the fact that the interviewee may deliberately try to deceive the interviewer. Eckman (1985) distinguishes between self-deception, where the interviewee lies to themselves, and other-deception, where they knowingly lie in order to conceal or falsify

Table 5.1 Inhibitors and facilitators of effective communication in interviews (Gorden 1975)

Factor	Subtype of factor	Examples
Inhibitors – make effective communication less likely	Unwillingness to give information	• Time demands • Threats to self-esteem • Threats to privacy
	Inability to give information	• Confusion • Mental state (e.g. stress) • Disability (e.g. memory problems)
Facilitators – make effective communication more likely		• The interviewer communicates expectations clearly • Appealing to the interviewee's sense of altruism • The interviewer offers sympathetic understanding • Catharsis – the interviewee feels relieved by talking about unpleasant experiences • Extrinsic rewards – the interviewee is offered additional inducement to co-operate

information. Both types of deception have the dual function of protecting the interviewee's self-esteem and avoiding external consequences such as punishment. Gudjonsson (1990) examined tendencies toward self- and other-deception in a number of offenders. He found that the highest levels of other-deception were for violent and sex offenders. He comments that such offenders apparently also engage in high levels of self-deception, being unwilling to admit that they have ever desired to rape or murder, even when it is clear they have intentionally done these things. In general, the more serious the offence, the greater the tendency of the offender to engage in deception. Possible reasons for this include not wanting to be branded an offender, not wanting to acknowledge what was done and not wanting to face the consequences of offending.

Interrogation

The purpose of an interrogation is to extract a confession from a suspect. Many police forces use one of a number of manuals for interrogators. These are typically based on the methods of experienced interrogators, rather than on systematic research. However, the methods employed are psychologically sophisticated and can involve deception, manipulation, pressure and persuasion. Some commentators (e.g. Zimbardo 1967) believe that such techniques are coercive and violate the rights of the suspect. Recently, a number of high-profile miscarriages of justice have highlighted the extent to which coercive interviewing can result in false confessions and wrongful convictions. This issue will be discussed below, following a consideration of some common interrogation techniques.

According to Gudjonsson (1992), the most authoritative guide to interview techniques is by Inbau et al. (1986), which is widely used in the US. They suggest that a successful interrogation consists of nine steps. The techniques contained in it are used by both police and military interrogators. Table 5.2 contains a summary of the interrogation procedures recommended by Inbau et al.

A number of researchers have directly examined the techniques used by the British police and concluded that there is evidence that officers make some use of persuasive tactics like those advocated by Inbau et al. Softley (1980) observed 218 interviews with suspects conducted by various English police forces. He found that 48 per cent of suspects

Table 5.2 Interrogation techniques (Inbau et al. 1986)

Step		Explanation
1	Direct positive confrontation	The suspect is told directly that they are considered to have committed the offence.
2	Theme development	The interrogator suggests to the suspect possible accounts of the crime, which minimise their involvement or culpability. The aim is to show sympathy and understanding.
3	Handling denials	The suspect is not allowed to repeatedly deny the offence. The interrogator interrupts denials to prevent the suspect gaining a psychological advantage.
4	Overcoming objections	The interrogator does not acknowledge reasons for the suspect's innocence. Once the suspect realises that objections get them nowhere, they stop making them.
5	Procurement and retention of suspect's attention	In order to avoid withdrawal on the suspect's part, the interrogator maintains physical proximity, good eye contact and uses the suspect's first name.
6	Handling suspect's passive mood	A continuation of step 4 in which the interrogator tries to facilitate a remorseful mood in the suspect, for example, by focusing on the victim's distress.
7	Presenting an alternative question	The suspect is presented with two accounts of the crime. Both are incriminating but one allows the suspect to explain *why* they committed the crime. Inbau et al. believe that this alternative is more attractive to the suspect.

Table 5.2 (Continued)	
Step	Explanation
8 Having suspect orally relate details of offence	Having accepted one of the accounts offered in step 7, the suspect gives an oral confession.
9 Converting oral into written confession	The oral confession is put down in writing in order to overcome a possible retraction by the suspect later.

made a full confession and 13 per cent made damaging and self-incriminating admissions. Persuasive techniques were used in 60 per cent of interviews. The most common technique was pointing to inconsistencies in the suspect's statement, which was used in 22 per cent of interviews. Other techniques included telling the suspect that there was compelling evidence against them (13 per cent) or hinting that further evidence was available (15 per cent). In 6 per cent of interviews, the officer minimised the seriousness of the offence and, in 7 per cent, the suspect was threatened with longer detention if they did not co-operate.

Interview procedures in the UK were greatly affected by the introduction of the **Police and Criminal Evidence Act** (PACE) in 1984, which limits the extent to which officers are allowed to use coercion during interrogations. Consequently, interviews are less likely to be conducted at night, are better recorded (i.e. tapes are used rather than written statements) and suspects are more likely to consult a solicitor before interrogation (Irving and McKenzie 1989). Moston (1990a) analysed 400 taped interrogations carried out by the Metropolitan Police and found that officers typically used one of two techniques, referred to as the inquisitorial and accusatorial strategies. The inquisitorial strategy aims to obtain information whereas the accusatorial strategy aims to extract a confession. Most officers used an accusatorial strategy in which the suspect was directly accused of the offence, the evidence against them was presented and then the accusation was repeated. Moston concluded that there had been a dramatic fall in the use of manipulative techniques, presumably as a result of increased legal restrictions on police behaviour. However, he suggests that the techniques currently used may increase the chance of a false confession from certain suspects (see below).

Pearse and Gudjonsson (1999) analysed interview recordings from eighteen serious crimes and found that the police tend to use six tactics in interrogations. These are outlined in Table 5.3.

Pearse and Gudjonsson found that the most frequently used tactics were robust challenge and intimidation. The use of these tactics tended to increase throughout the interview until the suspect confessed. Of the eighteen cases examined, ten resulted in a conviction. Interestingly, it was found that the tactics used by the police were related to the chance that the confession would be ruled inadmissible by the court. In four

Table 5.3 Police interview tactics (Pearse and Gudjonsson 1999)	
Tactic	*Explanation*
Intimidation	Intimidating the suspect by emphasising the seriousness of their situation, the experience of the officer and other factors.
Robust challenge	Disputing the suspect's account and accusing them outright of lying.
Manipulation	Minimising the seriousness of the offence and the suspect's degree of responsibility.
Questioning style	The use of leading questions, closed questions and multiple questions.
Appeal	Appealing to the suspect's good character and reassuring them.
Soft challenge	Introducing the suspect's version of events; speaking quietly.

out of six cases where intimidation had been used to an extreme level, the confession was ruled inadmissible.

Gudjonsson (1992) raises a number of problematic issues relating to police interrogation tactics. The first is that they use psychological techniques to coerce suspects into incriminating themselves and may use deceit and dishonesty, which raises ethical concerns. Second, interrogators tend to rely on 'lie signs' or body language that supposedly indicates the suspect is lying. Generally, however, such signs are very unreliable as evidence of lying. Third, the psychological manipulations of interrogators can influence the judgements of judges and jurors if the suspect's statement is used in evidence. Finally, the interrogation manuals used by the police tend to be based on experience rather than on controlled studies. This means that some of the claims about suspects' behaviour made in them have not been properly tested and may be of dubious value.

False confessions

The most problematic issue raised by the use of coercive interrogation tactics is that of false confessions. Cases like those of the Birmingham Six and the Guildford Four, in which innocent people were convicted of terrorist offences on the basis of false confessions, have brought this problem into the public eye over the course of the 1990s. Unfortunately, Gudjonsson (1992) points out that the police are generally reluctant to concede that false confessions happen and hence tend to over-rely on confessions as evidence of guilt.

Gudjonsson (1992) describes three types of false confession. These are outlined in Table 5.4

Because of the potentially disastrous consequences of a false confession, Gudjonsson highlights the importance of research into the circumstances under which they are likely to be obtained. He suggests that the circumstances surrounding potentially false confessions should be examined thoroughly in order to assess whether a confession or self-incriminatory statement is likely to have been coerced. Of particular interest are the factors outlined in Table 5.5

Although he concedes that PACE has improved police interviewing tactics, Gudjonsson points out that the probability of false confessions could be further reduced in a number of ways. In particular, vulnerable suspects are still not routinely identified, and their right to have an

Table 5.4 Types of false confession (Gudjonsson 1992)

Type of false confession	Description	Explanation
Voluntary	A person admits to an offence that they have not committed because they believe they have done it.	This type of confession is primarily associated with mental disorder. For example, a schizophrenic patient may admit to a murder they have merely heard about.
Coerced-internalised	A person is convinced by the police that they committed the crime, even though they did not.	This may happen if the person distrusts their own memory, for example, if they have amnesia caused by alcohol or a head injury. They come to rely on external sources (i.e. the police) for their memories.
Coerced-compliant	A person confesses to a crime that they know they did not commit.	This happens mainly because of coercive interrogation techniques. The person confesses to escape the pressure of the interview situation.

'appropriate adult' to help them is seldom exercised. Additionally, the legal system has been reluctant to acknowledge false confessions as a real problem and judges and police are still very sceptical when presented with evidence that a confession is false. This means that, despite the high-profile cases mentioned above, the problem of false confessions in police interviews has not yet been satisfactorily addressed.

Table 5.5 Important factors in assessing the reliability of confessions (Gudjonsson 1992)

Factor	Explanation
The defendant	Very young and very old suspects are more likely to produce false confessions, as are those with low IQ or psychological problems such as depression and schizophrenia.
Arrest and custody	Suspects arrested in the middle of the night or suddenly and violently are at a disadvantage, as are those interrogated at night or for long periods.
Mental and physical state	Confessions may be unreliable if the suspect was highly stressed, anxious, ill or intoxicated prior to or during interrogation.
Interrogative factors	Coercive, biased or leading interview tactics may result in false confessions from vulnerable suspects.

Progress exercise

Imagine that you have been asked to advise a lawyer who claims her client's retracted confession was false. Which aspects of the police investigation would you focus on?

NEGOTIATION

The police are occasionally involved in situations where an offender has taken people hostage and is threatening them with violence. According to some research, hostage incidents (in the US at least) are on the increase (Hammer et al. 1994). Mirabella and Trudeau (1981) surveyed twenty-nine hostage situations and found that they lasted between one and forty hours, the average being twelve hours. The reasons why a hostage situation might arise vary, but common themes include:

- A terrorist group takes hostages (e.g. by hijacking a plane) in order to draw attention to their cause or to ensure the release of specified persons in prison.
- Police are called to an incident (such as a domestic dispute) and their presence results in a barricade/hostage situation.
- A criminal takes hostages in the course of another crime (e.g. a bank raid that 'goes wrong'.
- A criminal takes hostages in order to extort money.

Approaches to crisis management (including hostage incidents) fall into two main camps. In the early days of crisis management, a 'surround and exterminate' approach dominated which involved a tactical (i.e. forceful) response. Many law enforcement professionals now favour a 'contain and negotiate' approach that attempts to resolve the situation with the minimum of bloodshed (Logan 1998). Many police forces in the US now have their own crisis management and hostage negotiation teams. The FBI set up its own Critical Incident Negotiation Team (CINT) in 1985 to operate on a national and international level.

The initial police response to a hostage incident is typically to contain and evacuate the immediate area and to gather as much intelligence about the hostage taker as possible. Negotiations can then begin. Most hostage negotiation teams in the US follow the principles initially developed by the Michigan State Police. This model of hostage negotiation has four stages:

- Introduction and establishing contact – the negotiators make contact with the offenders and establish their demands.
- Relationship building – the negotiators attempt to build a relationship with the hostage taker(s) characterised by trust.
- Problem negotiation – the negotiators attempt to secure the release of the hostages.
- Resolution – the situation is brought to a close.

Although it is always hoped that the situation will be resolved peacefully, it is acknowledged that the actions of the hostage taker may require a more forceful response and therefore hostage negotiators usually work closely with tactical teams who are ready to intervene if negotiations irrevocably break down.

There is a relatively large research literature concerning hostage negotiation. However, the vast majority of this is written by the police, for the police and is concerned with practical issues such as selection and training of negotiators. There has been a lack of controlled scientific research into the negotiation tactics that are most likely to produce satisfactory outcomes. Early research tended to focus on the psychological characteristics of the hostage taker. However, it has become clear that there is no 'typical' hostage taker and the focus of research has shifted towards the relationship between hostage taker and negotiator.

Donohoe and Roberto (1993) conducted a detailed analysis of negotiations in ten separate incidents. They found a significant relationship between the level of affiliation between negotiator and hostage taker and the outcome of the situation. That is, if the negotiators could develop a close and trusting relationship with the hostage taker, then the incident was more likely to be resolved peacefully. This is an important insight when it is considered that police officers vary in the degree of hostility they display towards the perpetrator. If they are a known criminal then the police attitude tends to be more hostile (Calhoun and Brooks 1997). This suggests that outcomes in hostage situations involving a known criminal are likely to be poorer unless officers are made aware of their biases and encouraged to modify them (Logan 1998).

Another factor that can influence the outcome of a hostage situation is the involvement of the media. Increasingly, our society is becoming media saturated and it is increasingly common in the US for news media to report hostage incidents from the scene as they happen. Because it is common for hostage takers to monitor media coverage of the situation police forces have begun to issue guidelines to media organisations as to how their coverage should be conducted. Typical guidelines might include:

- Avoiding speculation about the perpetrator's state of mind or history as this may inflame the situation.

- Providing no information about the activities of **SWAT** (Special Weapons and Tactics) or other tactical teams or even mentioning they are on the scene as this may cause the perpetrator to feel pressured.
- Avoiding mention of any senior officers who are on the scene as this may undermine the negotiator's authority.

Source: Based on a press release issued by the
Caddo-Bossier Sheriff's Office, 1997.

In conclusion, there are a number of factors that mediate the outcome of hostage-taking incidents, including the relationship between hostage taker and negotiator and the presence and activities of the media. Unfortunately, there has been a great lack of sound psychological research into the most effective means of conducting negotiations. This has been noted by a number of researchers and studies are currently being conducted into factors such as the psychiatric characteristics of hostage takers (Feldmann 2001) and the relational aspects of hostage negotiation (Logan 1998). Over the next few years, then, it can be expected that our knowledge of the psychology of hostage situations will improve.

Chapter summary

The police fulfil a wide range of functions in society but are chiefly concerned with enforcing the law and investigating offences. There is some evidence that people with particular personality characteristics are drawn towards police work but it is also fair to say that the characteristics of police work affect officers' personalities to a certain extent. Research into police interview techniques has raised a number of concerns, particularly over the extent to which manipulative and coercive tactics are employed. In some cases, the use of such tactics can result in a suspect confessing to a crime they did not actually commit. Many researchers now suggest that insufficient protection is given to vulnerable individuals who are at risk of making false confessions. Finally, police are increasingly called on to negotiate in hostage situations. Research has indicated that one of the crucial factors mediating a successful outcome is the quality of the relationship between negotiator and hostage taker but many other factors, including media presence, can also be involved. There is currently a lack of research concerning the factors that affect the outcomes of hostage incidents.

Further reading

G. Gudjonsson (1992) *The Psychology of Interrogations, Confessions and Testimony*. Chichester: Wiley. A classic text on interrogations and confessions. Chapter 12 contains detailed accounts of the cases of the Birmingham Six and the Guildford Four, two high-profile miscarriages of justice in which false confessions played a major part.

C. Hollin (1989) *Psychology and Crime: An Introduction to Criminological Psychology*. London: Routledge. Chapter 5 contains a thorough account of research into the police personality.

6

Offender profiling

◪ Principles of offender profiling

The purpose of a police investigation is to collect material evidence from the crime scene in order to reach some conclusions about the person(s) who might have committed that crime. Evidence might include fingerprints, fibres from clothes and blood. For example, consider the case of the Narborough Inquiry, the first case of **DNA profiling** used in a UK police investigation (see Figure 6.1).

The Narborough Inquiry may seem like a success, but blood testing every man was an inefficient method and it took months to complete

In 1983 a teenage girl was raped and murdered in the small town of Narborough. In today's society this may be nothing usual in itself, but in Narborough in 1983 crime was virtually unheard of. In 1986 another girl was raped and murdered. Using the revolutionary new technology of DNA profiling, forensic scientists found the same genetic material in the blood and semen left in both cases indicating it was the same man who had committed both cases (and therefore a serial killer). All 4,583 men in Narborough were tested and the police found their killer.

Figure 6.1 **The Narborough Inquiry (Salfati 1999)**

the analysis. What is needed is a method of narrowing down the suspect pool so that a smaller group of people can be tested. This is the purpose of offender profiling, originally developed by the FBI to understand if there is a link between what goes on at the crime scene and the type of person who commits the crime. Material evidence can be removed from the crime scene by the clever criminal, which can make police investigations very difficult. The criminal cannot, however, remove **behavioural evidence**. In a murder enquiry, behavioural evidence might include how the person was killed and where and how the body was left. This evidence is subtler than material evidence and might reveal something about the characteristics of the murderer. This chapter examines two major approaches to offender profiling and considers the problems that may arise from their use.

Progress exercise

If you read a newspaper report of a crime, or watch a TV programme such as *Crimewatch*, you will realise that often very few 'clues' are left behind at the scene of a crime. Apprehending offenders on the basis of such limited evidence can be an extremely difficult process and sometimes the police turn to psychologists for help. However, producing a 'psychological profile' of an offender may not be much easier. Take a newspaper report of a crime, and try to consider what information would be useful in trying to construct a psychological profile.

PRINCIPLES OF OFFENDER PROFILING

Media stereotypes of the criminological psychologist using insight and brilliant reasoning to 'get inside the head' of the criminal are more fiction than science. However, it can be very difficult to develop a clear understanding of offender profiling for a number of reasons (Ainsworth 2001). Profilers are often reluctant to publish their methods out of fear that they will be criticised or their methods plagiarised and there is considerable difference in practice between different profilers. In general, there is little common basis in the way that profiling is carried out, but all profiling generally has a common aim.

At the heart of profiling is the belief that characteristics of the *offender* can be deduced by a careful and considered examination of the characteristics of the *offence*. In other words profiling generally refers to the process of using all the available information about a crime, a crime scene, and a victim, in order to compose a profile of the (as yet) unknown perpetrator.

(Ainsworth 2001)

An example of this kind of approach can be seen in Figure 6.2.

Offender profiling was originally developed by the FBI, who set up their Behavioural Science Unit in the 1970s and eventually developed the set of profiling techniques known as **crime scene analysis**. However

---

Two cases of armed bank robbery have been committed, with four offenders in each, all masked and using guns. Money was taken. The police have no leads. The profiler would look for behavioural differences between the cases.

Case One	**Case Two**
Designated duties	No organisation
Semi-automatic machine-guns.	Shotguns
Targeted safe	Took available money
Used threats	Used physical violence
Disabled cameras	Left camera available

These behavioural differences between the two cases make it likely that different groups were responsible for each robbery. Evidence collected from previous investigations suggests that case one was carried out by professionals and case two by amateurs.

Professional	**Amateur**
Older	Younger
Links to organised crime	No links to organised crime
Not local	Live locally
History of non-violent crime	History of violent crime
Married	Not married

Figure 6.2 **A fictional case study (Salfati 1999)**

there have been documented cases of psychologists giving opinions to local police forces long before this (see Dr Brussel's profile of the New York City 'Mad Bomber' in Chapter 1). The FBI approach is only one of a number of different approaches to profiling which also includes diagnostic evaluation, an approach based on clinical judgements (similar to Brussel's profile) and **investigative psychology**, an approach developed in the UK (Wilson et al. 1997). The remainder of this chapter will focus on the FBI approach and investigative psychology, see Figure 6.3.

The FBI approach: crime scene analysis

In 1979, officers from the FBI Behavioural Science Unit (now called the Investigative Support Unit) started conducting extensive interviews with thirty-six serial killers and rapists, including some well-known criminals such as Charles Manson (Ressler et al. 1988). The results of these interviews, together with accumulated data from FBI investigations, suggested that murderers and rapists can be classified into different types according to motive, level of violence, likelihood of repeat offences and so on. The interview data eventually formed the basis of a national database, the Violent Criminal Apprehension Program (VICAP), set up in 1985 to develop psychological profiles of

---

Top-down approach

This is the approach developed by the FBI in the US, referred to as '**crime scene analysis**'. Evidence from the crime scene is compared to patterns from previous crimes in order to predict if any more crimes are likely and when and where they might take place.

Bottom-up approach

This is the approach used in the UK, principally developed by Professor David Canter (of Liverpool University), referred to as '**investigative psychology**'. People tend to act consistently in different situations (including crimes), so the way in which a crime was carried can be used to predict how an offender will act in other aspects of their life.

Figure 6.3 **Two major approaches to offender profiling (Boon and Davies 1992)**

criminals when combined with detailed police reports of the crime scene and the victim. Reports of murders are sent to the Investigative Support Unit where information is added to the database and offender profiles generated.

The FBI profiler gathers evidence from the crime scene (nature of attack, forensic evidence, medical reports on the victim, etc.) and uses the typologies developed by the Investigative Support Unit to advise police on location and likelihood of future offences, and the best interviewing strategies to use. The Investigative Support Unit have identified two different types of murderers, referred to as organised and disorganised murderers (Hazelwood 1987). The main characteristics of these different types of murderers are outlined in Table 6.1.

Table 6.1 Organised and disorganised murderers (Hazelwood 1987)

Type of murder	Likely characteristics of offender
Organised • Crime is planned • Attempt to control the victim • Leaves few clues at crime scene • Victim is a targeted stranger	• Above average IQ (possibly an underachiever) • Socially and sexually competent • Usually living with partner • Experiencing anger/depression at the time of the attack • Follows media coverage of attack
Disorganised • Little planning or preparation • Random, disorganised behaviour • Minimum use of constraint • Little attempt to hide evidence at crime scene	• Lives alone, near to crime scene • Sexually and socially inadequate • Experiences severe forms of mental illness • Physically or sexually abused in childhood • Frightened and confused at the time of the attack

Hazelwood also makes a distinction between different types of rapists. This approach is based on a classification system originally developed by Groth et al. (1977). The main characteristics of these different types of rapist are outlined in Table 6.2.

Evaluation of crime scene analysis

The UK-based investigative psychologist David Canter is sceptical of crime scene analysis for a number of reasons (Canter 2000). First, he argues that the type of information available at the crime scene is quite restricted and, as material is not collected under strict laboratory conditions, it could be potentially incomplete, ambiguous and unreliable. Consequently, any conclusions drawn from such information are necessarily speculative. Second, he argues that speculations about the criminal's motive are not much help to investigators trying to find a suspect. Essentially, Canter believes that the FBI approach is not really based in firmly established psychological principles. Following a crime, all profilers are presented with the same information. However, the individual profiler has to decide which behavioural evidence is important and may provide a link to the offender, and what is unimportant and can be discarded. The classification of offenders is made on the basis of this information. Therefore, the profile of the offender is based on the subjective judgements made by the profiler, rather than on a more scientific basis. As a result, Canter suggests that most of this kind of profiling is little more than informed speculation, similar to astrology in that guiding comments are offered which in reality are extremely ambiguous.

Finally, Canter argues that the typologies developed by the FBI for murderers and rapists are quite limited. They do not offer help for more common crimes such as car theft, burglary and assault. Additionally, the original study on which the FBI typologies were based may be fundamentally flawed. Canter points out that serial murderers are well known to be manipulative and attention seeking. For this reason, data obtained from them may be extremely suspect. Different interviewers may have obtained different information and it is possible that interviewers were manipulated somehow by the offenders.

However, as Ainsworth (2000) points out, crime scene analysis has been enormously influential. It has been successfully used in other countries including Canada and the Netherlands and has helped to solve

Table 6.2 Different types of rapist (Groth et al. 1977)

Type of rapist	Characteristics of attack
Power-reassurance	• Attack motivated by need to reduce doubt about sexuality • Use less force than other types of rapist • Attacks are carefully planned • Tends to reoffend in the same area • Keeps items of clothing as souvenirs
Power-assertive	• Typical 'acquaintance rape' • Initially friendly and non-threatening • Later behaviour changes to menacing • Rape is an expression of masculinity • Re-offences are rare
Anger-retaliatory	• Rape is an expression of anger and hostility towards women. • Victim is selected because they are symbolic of the offender's target of anger. • Attempts to humiliate victim • Tends to be unplanned with high levels of violence
Anger-excitement	• Sadistic motivation to produce suffering and fear • Attack is planned in advance, rehearsed and weapons selected before attack. • Uses extreme violence and torture, often resulting in death of victim • Victim is stranger • Keeps records of conquests

a number of high-profile cases. Although Canter questions the validity of crime scene analysis as an investigative tool, it does help the police to predict the level of violence, likelihood and timing of future offences. Such insights may be of considerable value and should not be neglected.

Offender profiling in the UK: investigative psychology

The UK approach to offender profiling began when Professor David Canter (then working at Surrey University) was approached by the Metropolitan Police to advise on whether psychology could be of any use to police investigations. In 1986, he became involved in a notorious case known as the 'Railway Rapist'. The profile developed by Canter helped the police arrest John Duffy, who was subsequently convicted of two murders and five rapes, and given seven life sentences. Canter's approach differs from the FBI approach in that he looks for ways in which the crime might mirror the behaviour of the offender in everyday life (this is known as the **criminal consistency hypothesis**). The idea is that offenders, like all people, act consistently over time and in different situations. Therefore, the way in which the crime is committed will reflect the everyday behaviour and traits of the offender. The consistency principle has been applied to two areas based in the psychological literature: interactions between the victim and the offender (interpersonal consistency) and the geographical area in which the offender commits his or her crimes (spatial consistency).

Canter and Heritage (1990) used the interpersonal consistency hypothesis to analyse the interactions between victim and offender in sixty-six cases of sexual assault carried out by twenty-seven different offenders. Their analysis showed that although there was no such thing as a 'typical rape', the most common characteristic of the attacks was not overt aggression or violence but a desire for some degree of sexual experience. Canter and Heritage highlight a number of possible links between behaviour during the attack and the characteristics of the offender:

- A rape where the offender does not initiate a high degree of sexual contact indicates someone with a low level of sexual activity in other areas of life. The profile would suggest a man living alone.
- The use of impersonal or degrading language would suggest a man who considers women to be objects of desire in other areas of life.

The profile would include failed domestic relationships or difficult relationships with women at work.
- An offender who warns a victim not to go to the police or destroys evidence would suggest that the offender had knowledge of police procedure from previous offences. The profile would include a criminal record.

One issue in consistency arises when behaviours apparently differ from one situation to another. If ten rape victims are gagged and an eleventh is bound, it might suggest that the last rape was committed by a different offender. However, focusing on a single behaviour like gagging or binding the victim ignores the meaning of that behaviour to the offender. Gagging and binding suggest a similar theme of control over the victim. Consequently, apparently different behaviours may just be different expressions of the same theme and therefore the same offender may have carried out the offences. Similarly, stalking and compliments may also seem like different behaviours but may represent the same theme of obsession (Salfati 1999). In this respect, Canter does not necessarily disagree with the FBI idea of classifying offenders, but believes that typologies should be based on the meaning of behaviours to the offender, not the overt behaviours themselves (Canter 2000).

One way of understanding the geographical patterns of offending is to consider spatial consistency, the idea that serial offenders operate in a limited area. Spatial consistency is based on the idea of mental maps. Mental maps are people's internal representations of the external world and are unique to each individual. For example, a taxi driver would have a very different mental map of an area to a non-driver. Criminals draw on their mental maps when planning and carrying out offences, so that areas in which offences take place have boundaries. These are unconscious and are a consequence of the offender's experience of their environment. They are likely to take into account such factors as escape routes, presence of CCTV and access to victims. Canter and Gregory (1994) identify two spatial patterns of offenders: **marauders** and **commuters**. A marauder uses a fixed base (often home) whereas the commuter travels to the crime location. If the pattern of offences suggests a detailed knowledge of the area, then it is likely the offender is a marauder and not a commuter. Therefore, the profile would include an estimation of the location of the offender's home base.

Between 1982 and 1986, the Metropolitan Police investigated twenty-four cases of sexual assault which took place near railways, the majority in North London. Between 1985 and 1986 three murders were committed, also by railways. Although the investigations were seriously hampered due to a lack of forensic evidence (the bodies had been burnt), the method of attack and the forensic evidence available suggested a link between the rapes and murders. The Metropolitan Police invited Canter to join the investigation, who developed the following profile using the procedures described above. Canter suggested the offender:

- lived near the first cases in 1983, possibly arrested in 1983, with partner (wife or girlfriend) and probably had no children,
- was in his mid to late 20s, approx 5'9" and right-handed,
- had a skilled or semi-skilled job, involving weekend work,
- was a quiet person, with one or two close male friends, little contact with women in the workplace and a detailed knowledge of the railway system,
- had considerable sexual activity prior to attacks and a previous criminal record, possibly for aggressive attacks under the influence of alcohol.

The profile enabled the investigation to proceed by narrowing down the list of suspects to those who fitted the profile. A police observation led to the arrest of John Duffy, who was eventually convicted of two murders and five rapes, and given seven life sentences. Originally Canter had very little material to work with, but by applying psychological principles to the police data produced a remarkably accurate profile.

Duffy lived in North London near to the first three rapes. He was recently separated from his wife and had no children. He was in his late 20s, right-handed and worked for British Rail as a carpenter. As Canter predicted, the bodies were burned in a deliberate move to destroy forensic evidence, a tip he picked up from the police when his house was searched following the rape of his wife.

In February 2001, Duffy's accomplice, John Mulcahy, was convicted of his part in seven rapes, three murders and five counts of conspiracy. Although victims had indicated an accomplice and Canter provided a second profile, a lack of forensic evidence prevented police from

> pursuing the case. Eventually Duffy agreed to name his accomplice leading to Mulcahy's arrest and subsequent prosecution.
>
> *Source*: David Canter (1994) *Criminal Shadows: Inside the Mind of a Serial Killer*. London: Harper Collins.

Figure 6.4 Canter's approach to profiling: 'The Railway Rapist'

Evaluation of investigative psychology

Canter believes that his approach has several advantages over crime scene analysis. First, his type of offender profiling draws directly on widely acknowledged psychological concepts (such as mental maps), which in Canter's view makes his approach a distinct branch of applied psychology. His choice of the term 'investigative psychology' to describe his approach represents a conscious effort to distance it from the work of the FBI. Second, there is no reason why Canter's approach should be limited to serious crimes such as murder and rape. In principle, his approach could also be applied to less serious but more common crimes (e.g. burglary and car theft). Finally, in investigative psychology there is less opportunity for the kind of subjective decision making inherent in crime scene analysis. Canter argues that his approach is more scientific than the FBI's. Consequently, his profiles are more useful as an investigative tool than crime scene analysis. That is, his profiles are more likely to help the police to actually catch the offender.

Psychological profiles provided by Canter have enabled the police to catch offenders in a number of high-profile cases including that of John Duffy (The Railway Rapist – see Figure 6.4). Such cases have attracted a high degree of media attention, which might give the impression that profiling in the UK is an unqualified success. However, there have also been a number of high-profile failures. A survey of detectives who had worked with offender profiling found that the advice given in the profile only helps to catch the offender in 3 per cent of cases (Copson 1995). Part of the problem may stem from a lack of consistency in the British approach. There are a number of individuals in the UK providing psychological profiles for the police with different backgrounds in psychology and psychiatry, each using his or her individual approach. Although Canter's approach is the most well known, there is no authority to impose a unified approach in the UK as there is in the US with the FBI. In fact there has been some remarkable squabbling between David Canter and another well-known UK profiler, Paul Britton, as to the best approach to take, which can only serve to damage the reputation of UK profiling (Ainsworth 2000).

Biases and pitfalls in offender profiling

At present, there are no universally accepted criteria for evaluating the success of offender profiling. For example, if a psychological profile was only 50 per cent accurate, but resulted in an arrest, would this constitute success or failure (Ainsworth 2000)? Some surveys have tried to establish the extent to which profiling is actually used and whether it has aided the investigation. In 1981, the FBI used psychological profiles in 192 cases. However, the profile was of direct help to the investigation in only 17 per cent of cases (Holmes 1989). More recently, the FBI has claimed an 80 per cent success rate in developing accurate profiles (Canter and Heritage 1990). In the UK, Copson (1995) surveyed forty-eight police forces using psychological profiles and found mixed results. In 83 per cent of cases the advice given by the profiler was found to be useful. However, it only offered direct help in solving the crime in 14 per cent of cases and only led to identifying the offender in 3 per cent of cases. As Canter (1989) notes, this type of survey data is somewhat superficial in that it does not reveal why offender profiling may or may not work.

The success of profiling may depend, in part, on how the profile is used by the police. At one extreme, the police may be extremely suspicious of 'outsiders' with no direct experience of investigative procedures and hence ignore the profile. At the other extreme, when the profile is used in isolation, there is rarely enough substantial evidence to direct an investigation (Jackson et al. 1997). Neither extreme is likely to produce results. In fact, disillusionment with psychological profiling in senior police officers may stem from a lack of understanding about both the aims of profiling and what it can achieve. Offender profiling has the potential to help police investigations by narrowing down the suspect pool. In this respect, Ainsworth (2000) draws attention to the Dutch Profiling Unit as a model of good practice. Police and profilers work together and the profile is never seen as a separate entity, but an investigative tool providing advice on how to proceed in a particular investigation.

There are, however, a number of practical and ethical dilemmas relevant to any type of profiling which must be thoroughly considered. There is a potential danger that investigations will target only the suspects who fit the description provided in the profile. Many writers point out the pitfalls of such an approach. Psychological profiles can only provide probabilities and may not be totally accurate. It should also be remembered that if police have a suspect who fits the profile, this person could be just one of many people who fit the profile. As Ainsworth (2000) notes, a profile does not 'prove' a suspect committed an offence and as such police should be cautioned against presuming guilt purely on the basis of a profile.

On a final note, one must consider how much responsibility the psychologist should carry for a miscarriage of justice in a case using a psychological profile. Harrower (1996) describes the worst case scenario in which profiling was used improperly, with one psychologist appearing in a court case as an expert witness in favour of offender profiling and another providing expert evidence against offender profiling.

Compare and contrast the British and American approaches to offender profiling.
What are the similarities and differences between each approach?

Progress exercise

Harrower (1996) concludes that offender profiling has undoubted potential if done in a methodical and scientific manner. However, at present its status is uncertain. Although police investigations are using psychological profiles, Copson (1995) suggests that in most cases the profile is not used as an investigative tool, but as expert reassurance.

Chapter summary

There is increasing use of psychological profiling by police in Europe and the US. The FBI's approach to profiling (crime scene analysis) attempts to assign an offender to one of a set of categories based on the type of offence they commit. Canter's approach in the UK (investigative psychology) has focused on a more individualistic approach. The way in which a crime is committed will reveal ways in which the offender behaves in other aspects of their life. Canter believes that the FBI's methods are speculative and not based in a scientific, psychological approach. In contrast, he argues that his approach offers more scope and scientific rigour by applying psychological principles (e.g. mental maps) to the behaviour of offenders. There are no satisfactory criteria by which to assess whether a psychological profile has helped a police investigation, so extravagant claims made for offender profiling should be treated with suspicion. Psychological profiles currently offer, at best, a small contribution to police work.

Further reading

Ainsworth, P.B. (2000) *Psychology and Crime: Myths and Reality*. Harlow: Pearson Education. See Chapter 6 for an accessible and lucid introduction to offender profiling.

Ainsworth, P.B. (2001) *Offender Profiling and Crime Analysis*. Cullumpton: Willan. This book is an in-depth and up-to-date account of offender profiling. Highly recommended for anyone wishing to find out more about offender profiling.

Britton, P. (1997) *The Jigsaw Man*. London: Bantam Press.

Canter, D. (1994) *Criminal Shadows: Inside the Mind of a Serial Killer*. London: Harper Collins.

Two books, written by the most well-known offender profilers in the UK, about their cases.

7

The psychology of testimony

◰ Cognitive processes and testimony
◇ Attribution theory and bias in eyewitness testimony
◪ Identification of suspects and events
◭ Aids to witness recall and recognition

Many people happen to witness a crime at some point. This could happen in many ways, for example, in a pub where an argument escalates into a fight and someone is assaulted or possibly a more serious crime such as the armed robbery of a bank. However serious the case, each witness will have important and perhaps crucial details of the event or the people involved. This information could be very important in helping the police solve the crime and apprehend the suspects.

Witnesses could be asked by the police to provide information in a number of ways (see Table 7.1)

In addition to providing police with information, a witness could be called into a court where legal professionals (barristers and solicitors) may wish to ask specific questions or to cross-examine the testimony of a witness. This chapter will consider three aspects of eyewitness memory: cognitive processes and testimony, variables influencing eyewitness memory and finally techniques used to improve eyewitness memory.

Table 7.1 Ways in which witnesses may assist the police	
Police interview	The witness is interviewed by the police to provide as many details of the event as they can.
Artist impression	A police artist gathers details from the witness about the facial features of the offender to produce a sketch.
Identikit and photofit	The witness is asked to pick out facial features (e.g. nose, chin) of the offender separately from a selection of facial features which are arranged to produce a whole face.
Identity parade	The witness is asked to identify the offender from a line-up of possible suspects.
Witness statement	A legal statement, jointly compiled by the witness and a police officer, signed by the witness as a definitive version of events.

COGNITIVE PROCESSES AND TESTIMONY

Psychologists have been studying memory since the late 1890s. In fact, two of the pioneers of psychology, William James (in the US) and Herman Ebbinghaus (in Germany) were developing theories of memory in the nineteenth century that are still relevant today. Hugo Munsterberg, an American psychologist, started applying psychological research into memory and other cognitive processes to testimony and jury decision making early in the twentieth century. Unfortunately, he was faced with a hostile legal profession who rejected his claims. Since the 1960s psychologists have conducted an enormous amount of laboratory-based research into memory. As Hollin (1995) notes, the memory of people who are eyewitnesses to crimes is an obvious real-life application of lab-based research.

Most people seem to think that our memory works passively like a video recorder. We can 'play back' information in exactly the same form that it was 'recorded', providing an accurate and objective record of the world. If our memory worked like this then eyewitness memory would not raise any issues. Witnesses would be able to provide accurate accounts of events with no loss of detail and identify suspects without any chance of error. Unfortunately, memory does not work like this. Witnesses can sometimes provide only hazy recollections of events, sometimes contradicting themselves and mistakenly identifying suspects.

For AS Psychology, you will have studied cognitive psychology, including memory, and some introductory research on eyewitness testimony (such as the work of Loftus). Imagine that you have witnessed a crime (e.g. an armed robbery in a shop). Using one or more of the theories you have studied from memory, consider how you would remember (or forget) the details of that crime. For example, you could consider:

- Models of memory (e.g. multi-store model, levels of processing, etc.)
- Theories of forgetting (e.g. trace decay, motivated forgetting, cue-dependent forgetting, etc.)
- The reconstructive nature of memory (e.g. schema theory)

Progress exercise

Four areas of psychological research can shed light on the cognitive processes behind eyewitness memory: the active nature of perception, the reconstructive nature of memory, theories of forgetting and theories of **social cognition**. This section will examine how these research areas can contribute to our understanding of the weaknesses of eyewitness testimony.

Active and selective perception

What does it mean to say that perception is an active process? Imagine if ten people were asked to describe a film they had just seen. It is probable that we would end up with ten rather different accounts. Some people will find the film more interesting than others; parts of the film may have personal relevance to some people, perhaps reminding them of their own experiences. In short, we bring a host of different factors to a situation, which will influence how we perceive what goes on. This is the 'active' part of human perception: we are biased in the way we process sensory information. It is important to appreciate that we are not aware of these biases, because cognitive processes are automatic and do not require conscious control. So when psychologists use the term 'active' to describe perception, they are suggesting that although the world we perceive appears to be 'out there', it is not independent of our cognitive processes. It is almost as if we perceive the world through psychological goggles, but are not aware they are present.

A number of factors influence perception. These include expectation, emotion, context and culture. For example, people tend to perceive TAI3LE as 'table' because of the context supplied by the letters. Alternatively, depressed people tend to process information in a biased way where they can only see negative aspects of their lives. In a similar way, when we witness a crime, our perception of that crime is not objective, but will contain elements of our interpretation of that event.

Reconstructive memory

The fact that perception is selective means that there will be gaps in people's memories. It appears that a fundamental feature of our cognitive system is to fill in these gaps using existing knowledge (Bartlett 1932). Bartlett's idea was that we can only understand new information by fitting it into the structure of our existing knowledge (or **schemas**). When this is difficult to do (for example, because new information is novel or complicated) it is likely that this new information will be forgotten or distorted. Once memory has been reconstructed it is not possible to recall the original version of events and it seems that the individual is completely unaware of any change. Although Bartlett's theory of reconstructive memory is widely accepted, it is a matter of some debate whether the original memory is irretrievably lost. Some theorists suggest that the original memory *can* be restored using the appropriate retrieval cues.

The reconstructive nature of memory is sufficient for everyday life where we do not need to know things in complete detail. When details are important the reconstructive nature of memory can become a problem. Elizabeth Loftus argues that, because of the reconstructive nature of memory, eyewitness memory is extremely unreliable. If a witness has gaps in their memory and is pushed to provide a comprehensive story, they could fill in these gaps with an 'imaginative reconstruction' based on experience or subsequent information heard in the media or suggested by an interviewer. Even if the witnesses were warned not to take into account subsequent material this would be impossible. As noted above, we are not aware of these automatic processes.

Forgetting

An understanding of forgetting is of crucial importance to eyewitness memory. If, for example, we believe that once we have forgotten something then that information is gone for good, this will influence how we approach eyewitnesses. If, on the other hand, we believe that once we have forgotten something, we can still retrieve that information with the help of a 'cue' then we will take a very different approach. There are many different theories of forgetting, but three of the major theories are trace-dependent forgetting, cue-dependent forgetting and motivated forgetting.

Trace-dependent forgetting

According to the theory of trace-dependent forgetting, the memory trace fades with time and, once forgetting has occurred, material has been lost from the memory system. If this theory is correct then eyewitnesses should be interviewed as soon as possible after the crime. This theory does have some experimental support (Jenkins and Dallenbach 1924), but research has also shown that it is not so much time, as what we do in this time, that is the crucial factor (Davies 1999).

Cue-dependent forgetting

According to the cue-dependent theory of forgetting, it is possible to access lost memories by using the right cues such as mood (state cues) and surroundings (context cues). The theory suggests that memories have not decayed but are present in the memory system, just not accessible. If this theory is correct then it should be possible to improve witness recall by using cues. This could involve asking the witness to recall their emotions and environment at the time of the crime. This theory has a great deal of experimental support (for example, see Aggleton and Waskett 1999). It has subsequently been developed into a special interview technique for use with eyewitnesses called 'cognitive interviewing' (see below).

Motivated forgetting

According to the theory of motivated forgetting, we repress disturbing or frightening memories because they cause high levels of anxiety. Therefore, if an eyewitness cannot remember many details of a violent crime, this information might still be present in the memory system but unavailable. If this is the case, how do we get to these memories? Some psychologists believe that it is possible to uncover these memories using hypnosis. Many psychologists are sceptical of this idea and technique (see below), but it remains very difficult to test experimentally.

Social cognition

In addition to studying perception, memory and forgetting, psychologists have also investigated social cognition, that is, how cognitive processes operate in social situations. A major part of social cognition looks at the way social information is processed and, in particular, at biases in the way we process social information. Research in this area has led to advances in the ways that social phenomena such as stereotypes, prejudice and identity have been thought about. Since crime itself is a social phenomenon, insights into social information processing could be usefully applied to improve our understanding of crime. Perhaps the area of social information processing most relevant to eyewitness memory is attribution theory.

ATTRIBUTION THEORY AND BIAS IN EYEWITNESS TESTIMONY

Attribution theory is concerned with how people in social situations work out the causes of their own and others' behaviour, that is, to what causes we *attribute* behaviour. Models of attribution have considered the 'rules' by which we work out whether behaviour is caused by factors internal to the person (dispositional factors) or external to the person (situational factors). Making an internal or **dispositional attribution** involves saying that something about the person themselves (such as their personality) is the cause of their behaviour. Making an external or **situational attribution** involves saying that something outside of the person (i.e. the situation) is the cause of their behaviour. For example, if we witness someone being angry we have two choices over attribution. We could make a dispositional attribution by saying that they are a bad-tempered person. An alternative could be to say they are reacting to a very frustrating circumstance, which would be a situational attribution. Research has shown that we are biased in the way we make attributions, sometimes towards situational attributions and at other times towards dispositional attributions.

How can attributional biases be applied to eyewitness testimony? Remember that recall of a crime is not an impersonal and objective record of events, but a record of a person's interpretation of what happened. Biased attributions made when a crime was originally witnessed will be encoded along with other details. When a witness is asked to recall details of a crime, these biased attributions will also be recalled. An understanding of three different types of attributional bias can be applied to eyewitness memory. These are the fundamental attribution bias, the actor-observer effect and the self-serving attribution bias.

Fundamental attribution bias

The **fundamental attribution bias** refers to a tendency to make situational attributions for our own behaviour and dispositional attributions for others' behaviour. A good example of this kind of error can be seen in the just-world hypothesis. The just-world hypothesis refers to the belief, held by some people, that the world is a safe and just place. Lerner (1980), who coined the term, suggests that 'some individuals have a need to believe they live in a just world where people generally get what they deserve and deserve what they get'. The effect of the just-world hypothesis on victims of crime was discussed in Chapter 2. In judging the victims of crime, people with a strong belief in a just world show a fundamental attribution error. That is, they judge victims of crime as being responsible for their own fate (a dispositional attribution) rather than as unfortunate victims of circumstances beyond their control (a situational attribution).

People with a strong belief in a just world can have their fundamental attribution error strongly challenged by meeting innocent victims of crime (such as rape victims) as the experiences of such people suggest that the world is not a just place. Klinke and Meyer (1990) suggest that under such circumstances people do not want to give up their belief and so can do one of two things: remove the victim's suffering or blame the victim for their own fate. Since it is not possible simply to remove a rape victim's suffering, there is a tendency to subject them to derogation and blame. That is, they are judged to have brought their misfortune on themselves. In this way the person who believes in a just world can maintain his or her dispositional attribution as the victim actually 'deserved' to be raped. Dispositional attributions can be maintained in a number of ways, such as by blaming the victim's appearance (e.g. revealing clothing), behaviour (e.g. walking alone at night) or personality (e.g. attention seeking).

However, belief in a just world does not have to result in victim derogation. Lerner and Miller (1978) suggest that three factors determine whether a victim will be derogated:

- The victim must be innocent. If the victim is obviously responsible for their actions there is no violation of the just world in the first place.
- Victims who are highly attractive or who have high social status are derogated less.
- If the observer identifies with the victim (e.g. they are also a rape victim) it is less likely that they will derogate the victim.

In summary, when belief in a just world is challenged by innocent victims who do not seem to deserve their misfortune, the just world can be restored by derogating the victim (a dispositional attribution). Placing blame on the victim makes it seem as if they are getting what they deserve and that the world is a just place after all.

The actor-observer effect

Another kind of attributional bias is the actor-observer effect. This refers to a tendency to attribute our own behaviour to situational or external factors and the behaviour of others to internal or dispositional factors. An example of this kind of attributional bias can be seen in **hedonic relevance**. Hedonic relevance refers to the kind of attributional biases we make when something has particular personal relevance (Brewer 2000). For example, if we had a car crash involving another driver, we are likely to make dispositional attributions about the other driver (*they* were driving too fast) and situational attributions about our own driving (the road was icy).

A study by Walster (1966) shows that attributions made by observers can change depending on the consequences of the action. Participants were presented with a story about a car rolling down a hill. The stories had a variety of different endings and the participants were asked to explain why the car was rolling down the hill. Where there was little injury or damage, observers did not tend to place responsibility with the car owner. Participants suggested reasons such as mechanical failure (a situational attribution). Where there were higher levels of injury or damage, observers tended to blame the car owner, for example for not applying the handbrake properly (a dispositional attribution). These results suggest that the testimony of witnesses to an accident is not an objective, accurate record of events but is subject to social information processing biases.

Self-serving attribution bias

Self-serving attributional bias refers to the tendency to attribute our successes to dispositional factors and our failures to situational factors. A study by Scully and Marolla (1984) showed that men who have been convicted of rape tended to engage in this kind of attributional bias. 114 convicted rapists were interviewed to find out how they justified or explained their actions. 40 per cent of interviewees blamed the victim, portraying her as a willing seductress. The remaining 60 per cent blamed their actions on drugs or alcohol. In both cases the rapists were making attributions that shifted responsibility away from themselves on to external factors (either the victim or intoxicants). It seems that the purpose of self-serving bias is to maintain a positive self-image. By making dispositional attributions, the rapists could maintain a view of themselves as a 'nice person' despite the fact they had been convicted.

Attribution bias and witness testimony

What do these attributions suggest about eyewitness testimony? Research suggests that attributional biases will influence how an event is interpreted. The implication is that witnesses can only describe an interpretation of a crime, unwittingly suited to their own needs and biases. Research into the fundamental attribution error would suggest that an individual with a strong belief in a just world would recall events in such a way as to suggest that responsibility for events should lie with the victim and not the suspect. The principle of hedonic relevance would suggest that people involved in accidents tend to bias their testimony to shift responsibility on to the situation or other people. When others are involved in accidents we are more likely to place responsibility with the person involved if there is a high level of injury or damage. It seems as if witnesses to accidents, whether they are involved or not, produce testimony which is highly subjective and open to bias.

IDENTIFICATION OF SUSPECTS AND EVENTS

Psychological research has shown eyewitness memory is not infallible but is prone to error and reconstruction. Psychologists have carried out extensive research to investigate exactly which factors lead to errors in eyewitness memory. These can be grouped in terms of the three stages of memory: acquisition, retention and retrieval.

Acquisition

Acquisition refers to the stage where memories are encoded. In terms of eyewitness memory that means actually witnessing a crime. Three factors have been identified which affect eyewitness memory when the event was witnessed: time (duration and time of day), the level of violence and the use of weapons.

Time factors

As common sense might predict, the longer the time spent witnessing an event, the better our memory for that event. Support for this comes from a study by Clifford and Richards (1977) where a target person was exposed to a group of policemen for fifteen seconds. The same person was exposed to another group of policemen for thirty seconds. Unsurprisingly, results showed that accurate recall was much better for the group exposed for thirty seconds.

Regarding the time of day, Kuehn (1974) found that the most detailed witness statements were taken when incidents took place in full daylight or at night. The least complete witness statements were taken at twilight. These results are somewhat surprising. It might be expected that the best witness statements are produced under the best viewing conditions. If this were the case then the best statements would be produced in the day, the next best at twilight and the poorest at night. So how can the results of Kuehn's study be explained? One possibility is that detailed witness statements are produced in the day because witnesses have good viewing conditions. At night witnesses are aware that viewing conditions are bad and so make a special effort to compensate for this with increased vigilance and attention, in turn producing detailed witness statements. During twilight witnesses overestimate viewing conditions and, because they have not made any efforts to compensate, the witness statements produced at this time are not as detailed.

A related question concerns whether witnesses can accurately estimate how long an incident lasted. It appears that most people tend to overestimate the amount of time that an incident lasts. Buckhout et al. (1975) devised an ingenious study to demonstrate this principle. They staged an assault on a professor in front of a packed lecture theatre. The dumbfounded students made perfect naïve witnesses. Students on average estimated that the incident lasted eighty-one seconds. However, the attack lasted only thirty-four seconds, so the students overestimated the length of the incident by about two and a half times. Why is this? Many people report witnessing dramatic events – a car crash or dropping an expensive vase perhaps – as if they were in 'slow motion'. Perception of time is variable and it seems that emotional events, such as witnessing an assault, can lead to time distortion such as overestimating the length of such events.

Violence distraction

Another factor affecting eyewitness memory occurring at the time when the event was witnessed is the level of violence. In general, research has shown that people have a better memory of non-violent events than violent events. This was demonstrated in a study by Clifford and Scott (1978). Participants were shown one of two short films. Both films involved the same people, but one film was violent (with scenes of physical assault) and the other was not. After watching the film, participants' recall was tested. The results showed that recall was significantly poorer for participants who had watched the violent film.

Further evidence for this effect, called '**violence distraction**' comes from a study by Clifford and Hollin (1981). They compared the effects on eyewitness recall of two types of distraction: violence and companions. Participants were shown one of six videotaped scenes. Three of these showed a violent incident in which a woman was attacked and her bag stolen. In each scene the male attacker was either alone, with two companions or with four companions. The remaining three scenes showed the same people but in non-violent incidents. The results showed that recall was significantly worse for the violent scenes. In the non-violent films, the number of companions present made no difference to recall. However, in the violent scenes recall became worse as the number of people increased.

One explanation for these results comes from a psychological principle called the Yerkes-Dodson Law. This states that moderate levels of arousal lead to the best performance and high levels of arousal lead to lower levels of performance. It might be that seeing violence causes such a high level of anxiety/arousal that memory is impaired. However, this is not the only possible explanation. Other research has shown that in violent incidents, witnesses tend to focus on weapons at the expense of other aspects of the situation. This phenomenon is referred to as 'weapon distraction' or 'weapon focus'.

Weapon focus

Weapon focus was demonstrated in an experiment by Loftus et al. (1987). Participants were shown a film in which a customer in a restaurant was holding either a gun or a cheque. Participants in the 'cheque' condition were much more accurate at identifying the customer and other details about the film than participants in the 'gun' condition. It is possible that in these terrifying situations, the attention of the witnesses is drawn to the weapon explaining why their memory for other events is less clear.

A further question is whether weapon focus is relevant to only guns or whether it applies to other weapons. A study by Maass and Kohnen (1989) suggests that it does. Participants were approached by a female experimenter holding either a syringe or a pen. When participants were subsequently asked to identify the experimenter who had approached them, those in the 'pen' condition were much more accurate than those in the 'syringe' condition. Research into violence distraction and weapon focus, then, suggests that witnesses to violent crimes involving weapons tend to produce less accurate testimony than witnesses to non-violent crimes.

Retention

Retention refers to the period between witnessing an event and subsequently retrieving that memory. Psychological research has investigated two factors that might be relevant to this: the length of time between witnessing a crime and subsequent retrieval and discussion of the witnessed events with others.

Memories seem to fade with time, a process which psychologists call 'trace-dependent' forgetting. It is widely believed that long-term memories are stored in the brain as circuits of neurones. When these circuits are not activated for long periods (i.e. when we do not use these memories), the connections between them weaken to the point when the circuit is broken and the information is lost or forgotten. According to this principle it would be expected that memory of crimes would fade when there is a long delay between witnessing a crime and retrieval. In general, this seems to be the case but there is one major exception: memory for face recognition does not seem to fade to the same degree as memory for events and details (Ellis 1984). Consequently, even if an eyewitness can not provide a detailed account of a crime in a police interview, they may still be able accurately to help identify suspects by helping with artist impressions, photofits or identity parades.

Other factors that occur prior to retrieval also have an effect. One such factor is the discussion of events by witnesses with people such as friends, family and other witnesses. Alper et al. (1976) investigated the effects of discussion prior to retrieval by staging a theft in a lecture theatre and then asking the students to act as witnesses. Recall of events was first tested individually and then followed by a group discussion of events with other witnesses. Following this discussion, recall was tested again based on group, rather than individual answers. Results showed that after the discussion, recall was more complete (a good thing) but tended to contain details that did not actually happen (a bad thing). So does discussing the event produce better or worse testimony? A study by Hollin and Clifford (1983) investigated this question. Witnesses to a staged event gave individual recall, then took part in a group discussion. Prior to the discussion, two of the witnesses were identified by the experimenter's assistant as experts in eyewitness recall. These two individuals were actually accomplices of the experimenters who deliberately gave wrong answers. When individual recall was re-tested after discussion, results showed that participants had altered their initial answers to conform to the wrong details given by the confederates. The results of this study suggest that group discussion with other witnesses prior to retrieval can adversely affect the accuracy of subsequent recall of events.

Retrieval

Retrieval refers to the stage in which memories are accessed. In terms of eyewitness memory, this is usually when the witness is required to provide evidence in one form or another. Retrieving memories can involve recalling details of an event in a police interview or recognising a face from a 'still' caught on a security camera (camera footage is turned into a photograph). Most of the research in this area has investigated the effect of leading questions and misleading information on eyewitness memory. Elizabeth Loftus, a leading American researcher into eyewitness memory, suggests that the form in which questions are asked will influence what is remembered. Leading questions are skilfully employed by both police and barristers to achieve this end. Evidence comes from two classic studies carried out in the 1970s by Loftus and Zanni (see key research summary p. 168) and Loftus and Palmer (1974).

Loftus and Palmer (1974) showed participants a film of a car crash and asked them to assess the vehicles' speed at the time of impact. The critical question was: 'How fast were the cars going when they *hit*?' For other groups, 'hit' was replaced with '*smashed*' or '*bumped*'. Results showed that the '*smashed*' group estimated an average speed of 40 mph, the '*bumped*' group estimated an average speed of 38 mph and the '*hit*' group estimated an average speed of 34 mph.

How can these results be explained? There are two possibilities. One is that the participants were responding to **demand characteristics** (that is, providing the answer that they thought the experimenters expected) and the other is that memory was undergoing a change (reconstructing what was encoded). Loftus and Palmer attempted to answer this question with a second part to their experiment. One week later participants were asked whether they had seen any broken glass in the film (there was none). 32 per cent of the '*smashed*' group said 'yes' compared to only 14 per cent of the '*hit*' group. According to Loftus, these results suggest that misleading questions cause a reconstruction of events so that original material is lost from memory.

Loftus's argument suggests that recall of the original event is practically impossible. Not all researchers agree with this interpretation. An alternative is that misleading information co-exists in memory with the original events. According to this argument, recall of the original event is possible if the appropriate retrieval cues are used (Hollin 1995).

Other researchers have questioned the **ecological validity** of laboratory studies of eyewitness memory. Participants in laboratory studies may differ from real witnesses in a number of ways. In Loftus's studies, participants viewed films and not real events. Laboratory studies fail to recreate the emotional impact of witnessing a real crime. For example, real witnesses may be highly anxious.

In a field study, Yuille and Cutshall (1986) interviewed eyewitnesses who had seen two people shot in broad daylight. They found that witnesses were able to produce accurate and detailed information about the shooting and leading questions did not produce subsequent errors in recall. Further research has identified that some conditions are more likely than others to result in reconstructive memory errors. These are listed in Figure 7.1.

Psychological research and the legal system

The research discussed above has shown that eyewitness memory is prone to error and perhaps not as reliable as some people might have thought. How could this information be used? Psychologists come into contact with the police and legal professions in two ways. First, psychologists are employed by the police in an educational role to advise officers on eyewitness memory. They address issues such as the reliability of testimony and how to improve interview techniques to

- Leading questions at the time of recall produce more errors in laboratory studies than in real-life crime studies.
- If the event was accurately witnessed (i.e. a clear view of events in broad daylight) then leading questions are less likely to produce errors in eyewitness memory.
- Errors in eyewitness memory are also less likely if misleading information is blatantly incorrect.
- Witnesses are more easily misled if misleading information is peripheral to the main event, if misleading information is given after a long delay and if witnesses are not aware they may have reason to mistrust information.

Figure 7.1 **Summary of research into the effects of misleading questions (Eysenck 1993)**

improve accuracy. Second, psychologists are sometimes asked to appear in court as 'expert witnesses' where they explain to the jury just how reliable (or not) eyewitness memory can be or possibly comment on the reliability of one particular witness. However, it is argued by some legal professionals that juries have an intuitive understanding of human behaviour and do not require specialised psychological knowledge.

Progress exercise

Imagine that you had to aid a police investigation. What advice would you give?

Go back to the beginning of **Identification of suspects and events**. For each of the sections: acquisition, retention and retrieval consider what practical advice could be given to police officers to minimise error in eyewitness memory and gain the most reliable testimonies.

AIDS TO WITNESS RECALL AND RECOGNITION

Although most research has highlighted the problematic nature of eyewitness memory, this knowledge can also be used to improve the memory of witnesses. This section will examine police procedures used to recall the details of a crime or to identify criminals. This will include a discussion of the ways in which psychological research can help to improve these techniques.

Identity parades

In an identity (or ID) parade, the suspect stands in line with a number of innocent foils (members of the public who have volunteered or been contacted by the police). The witness is asked to view each face in turn and to make a positive identification if they recognise that person as the one seen in the original event perpetrating or assisting in a crime. Despite the presence of regulations designed to ensure fair conduct, mistakes are still made that sometimes result in a wrongful conviction. Witnessing a crime can be a very stressful experience and viewing conditions are often less than perfect, yet witnesses can be very confident in their ability to recognise a face.

Some of the same factors affecting eyewitness memory in general (see above) are also relevant to ID parades. Research has shown that memory may deteriorate when there is a long gap between witnessing an event and subsequent recall, although the effect is less marked with recognition of faces. Another relevant factor is the emotional state of the witness. Stressful events, especially those involving violence or weapons, reduce the reliability of memory. Psychologists have also identified some factors that are specific to ID parades. These include showing the witness 'mugshots' of suspects prior to the ID parade, the composition of the line-up and the tendency of witnesses to ignore instructions.

Bruce (1988) has identified several cases in which a witness has made a positive identification of a suspect who has then produced an alibi. It has turned out that the witness has been shown photographs of the suspect prior to the ID parade. In these cases, the identification has been made on the basis of familiarity and the witness is unable to distinguish whether the face was recognised from the original incident or the subsequent photographs. If a witness has been shown a photograph of the suspect at any time before an ID parade, the validity of the whole exercise must be called into question.

The most important factor in the composition of the ID parade is the appearance of the foils. In the UK, seven foils are usually used but the critical issue is not the number of foils but whether they resemble the suspect (Ainsworth 2000). If an identity parade has seven foils, only four of which resemble the suspect, then the witness is likely to discount the foils that do not resemble the suspect. Under these circumstances the ID parade might as well only have the four foils that actually resemble the suspect. As Ainsworth points out, a line containing five foils who closely resemble the suspect is fairer than a line up containing seven foils where only four resemble the suspect. Brigham and Pfeiffer (1994) refer to the number of foils who resemble the suspect as the 'functional size' of an ID parade in contrast to the actual number of foils.

Most police stations in the UK which use ID parades on a regular basis have a register of volunteers with details of physical characteristics. In this way, it is possible to choose foils that physically resemble the suspect and thus increase the functional size of the parade. Some stations operate a system where fifteen to twenty volunteers who match the physical characteristics of the suspect are invited to attend the parade. When these volunteers arrive, a police officer selects only the six or seven individuals who most closely match the suspect to take part in the line up.

Even if the foils resemble the suspect in physical appearance, this does not discount the possibility that the witness is using some other means of recognition (for example, recognising the clothes of the suspect, rather than the face). One possibility is that the witness is more likely to identify the person displaying outward signs of nervousness (sweating, trembling, etc.) on the basis that they are more likely to be guilty (Ainsworth 2000). However, these signs may not necessarily indicate guilt. It is entirely reasonable to expect someone who has been wrongfully arrested and accused to be extremely nervous when appearing in an ID parade. Psychologists are faced with a methodological dilemma when trying to assess the impact of non-verbal cues (like nervousness) on ID parade recognition. It is not possible to generate in laboratory or mock ID parade studies the level of fear and anxiety that an innocent person would experience in situations such as this. Neither would it be ethical to subject somebody to this kind of experience without their consent. In conclusion, this point is necessarily speculative. There is no current evidence concerning whether a nervous person is more or less likely to be picked out when they have been wrongly accused.

The final problem stems from the procedure used in which the witness has to view the whole parade at once. Thomson (1995) found that some witnesses do not follow the instructions they are given. Instead of studying the individual faces of the people in the parade to see if they recognise them, they view the parade as a whole. They select people on the basis of whether they fit into an image in their memory, discounting those who do not fit and choosing the person whose appearance is most similar to this image. Recognition is being made on a probabilistic basis rather than on a definite positive identification.

One solution to this problem has been described by Cutler and Penrod (1995). They tested an alternative procedure in which the witness views one face at a time rather than the whole parade. After each face has been viewed, the witness indicates whether they recognise the face as the criminal. However, they are not told how many faces they will have to view. This procedure forces the witness to make a positive identification on the basis of facial recognition rather than on a rough probabilistic basis. Results showed this technique reduces the number of false positive identifications (where a foil is identified as the criminal), making it more reliable than the traditional ID parade.

So in conclusion, what advice can psychologists offer to the police regarding ID parades? First, under no circumstances should witnesses be shown photographs of suspects prior to the ID parade. Second, only foils that are similar in appearance to the suspect should be used in the line-up. Finally, instructions given to the witness should emphasise that they should view each face one at a time and not view the parade as a whole.

Indentikit and photofit

A general problem for witnesses is that it can be hard to describe a face to the level of detail required by the police. A related problem for the police is that artist impressions are time consuming and expensive to produce. Identikit and photofit techniques were developed in response to these problems. They allow witnesses to construct a face using either drawn or photographed features. The idea behind these techniques is that we recognise a whole face by breaking it down into its constituent parts (eyes, nose, mouth, etc; see Penry 1971). In both identikit and photofit, the witness constructs a face feature by feature (e.g., chin, eyes, hairline, etc.) until the whole face is complete. For each separate feature the witness is given a choice and has to choose the one that matches their memory. For example, when choosing the chin, the witness may be shown forty different types of chin and asked to choose the one that shows the closest likeness to the face they are trying to construct. Identikit refers to an early version using line drawn features and photofit refers to the later version using photographed features (see Figure 7.2).

The most important issue surrounding the use of identikit and photofit is whether they help the witness accurately to reconstruct the faces of suspects. A study by Laughery and Fowler (1980) compared the use of identikit with artists' impressions. Pairs of participants were asked to be 'witnesses' and given several minutes to view a target person they would later describe. One of the participants worked with a police artist and the other participant worked with the identikit technician. A team of judges then rated how similar the artist impression and the identikit construction were to the target person. The results showed the artist impressions to be significantly better than the identikit constructions. Photofit did not fare much better. Davies et al. (1978) carried out a similar study but compared photofit constructions with sketches produced by the witnesses themselves. The results

Identikit

Source: Ellis et al. (1975)

Photofit

Source: Sergent (1984)

Figure 7.2 **An example of a face reconstructed by a witness using identikit and photofit techniques (Reproduced with permission from the** *British Journal of Psychology* **© British Psychological Society)**

showed that the sketches were rated by participants as more similar to the target person than the photofit constructions.

The results of these studies indicate that identikit and photofit have limited usefulness as facial construction techniques. The question is, why? Bruce (1988) identifies a number of problems with these techniques that may explain why they fared so poorly in studies. First, in photofit there are a limited number of face shapes and features to choose from and so the one that is chosen will never be an exact match. Second, there is a serious problem with the nature of the task itself. Identikit and photofit are based on the notion that we recognise faces by breaking them down into their constituent parts. Subsequent research has shown that this is not the case. We do not process features separately but in parallel. In other words, we do not recognise features separately but at the same time. Additionally, research indicates that faces are not just recognised on the basis of the features themselves but also the relationship between these features (e.g. the distance between nose and mouth).

Does this mean that identikit and photofit are of no use at all? Some research has considered how they can be improved. It seems that some features are more important than others in recognising faces. Following this principle, the photofit (or identikit) technician should always start with the face and hair outline, followed by the eyes and mouth, the least important feature being the nose. Another technique based on the idea of cue-dependent forgetting is to 'reinstate the context' (see the discussion below of the 'cognitive interview'). The idea is to use cues to improve facial recall by asking witnesses to picture the background as well as the face and to imagine themselves back in the place where the incident took place.

Bruce (1988) concludes that the photofit system does have some potential but only if it incorporates new theoretical ideas from research on facial recognition. She suggests an improvement would be to use computerised systems to blend features into one another and programmed to take account of the relationships between features. This has now been implemented in the form of 'videofit' techniques but it appears that little research has yet been conducted to ascertain whether they produce reconstructions that are more accurate than photofit.

The cognitive interview

The traditional technique used by the police for witness interviews (referred to as the standard interview procedure, see Chapter 5) involves a period of free recall followed by specific questions by the police officer. Research by Elizabeth Loftus has cast some doubt over the validity of this procedure. In particular, there is a danger that leading questions may cause memory distortion (see Chapter 5 for a discussion of the standard police interview).

Geiselman et al. (1985) suggest that interview techniques should incorporate some basic psychological findings about memory. Research into cue-dependent forgetting has shown that memory traces contain many different types of information: some internal factors such as mood and psychological state and some external cues such as smell and colour of surroundings. According to the encoding specificity principle, the retrieval of a memory trace is more likely if the information in a cue overlaps with information in the memory trace. Retrieval can be improved by using as many cues as possible. The implication for police procedure is that a witness interview should use cues to stimulate memory whilst, at the same time, avoiding leading questions.

The cognitive interview was developed by Geiselman as an alternative to the standard interview procedure. It takes into account the psychological findings about cue-dependent forgetting outlined earlier. The four stages of the cognitive interview are designed to stimulate as many cues as possible in order to maximise different retrieval routes (see Figure 7.3).

Several questions must be asked of the cognitive interview: is it more effective than the standard interview, does it improve recall and does it reduce error? In response to these questions, a lab study by Geiselman et al. (1986) compared a cognitive interview with a standard police interview and a hypnotic interview. The standard police interview produced on average 29.4 correct witness statements, the cognitive interview an average of 41.1 correct statements and recall under hypnosis produced an average of 39 correct statements. The cognitive interview produced a 30 per cent improvement in recall with no increase in incorrect responses. Under laboratory conditions, it seems that the cognitive interview can certainly produce more correct details without increasing witness error.

However another lab study by Fisher et al. (1987) using an enhanced cognitive interview, found a 23 per cent improvement in correct witness

- Reinstate the context: the witness thinks back to the crime scene and imagines what the environment looked like and how they were feeling at the time.
- Events are recalled in reverse order.
- The witness reports everything they can think of, no matter how fragmented that memory might be.
- The witness tries to describe events from someone else's point of view.

Figure 7.3 **The four stages of the cognitive interview (Geiselman et al. 1985)**

statements but also a 28 per cent increase in incorrect statements. Eysenck and Keane (1995) suggest that the reason for the high number of errors was that the study was carried out under artificial lab conditions. In a real-life test, Fisher et al. (1990), trained detectives from the Miami Police Department to use the cognitive interview. Police interviews with eyewitnesses and victims were videotaped and the total number of statements was scored. A second eyewitness was then asked to confirm whether these were true or false. Compared to the standard procedure used, the cognitive interview produced a 46 per cent increase in recall and 90 per cent accuracy. With real-life witnesses, therefore, the cognitive interview has been shown to be more effective than the standard police interview, producing higher recall and reducing errors.

Forensic hypnosis

Hypnosis has been used in the United States since 1907 in the belief that it can aid the recall of witnesses and victims of crimes. In the UK hypnosis is not so popular, but nonetheless still used by some police forces. When hypnosis is used in this context, it is known as **forensic hypnosis** to distinguish it from hypnosis in a therapeutic or entertainment setting. Wagstaff (1983) defines forensic hypnosis as 'hypnosis applied to the collection of evidence for judicial purposes'. As such, it has a different aim from hypnosis used in therapeutic settings. The aim of forensic hypnosis is only to gather evidence; any emotional benefits are incidental. In a therapeutic setting, the primary aim of hypnosis (certainly to those from a psychodynamic orientation) is for emotional benefit: the lifting of repression from memories and so on.

In the UK, hypnosis is carried out by qualified psychologists employed by the police. In the US hypnosis is carried out by police officers trained in hypnosis. Although the profession of the hypnotist may differ, the techniques used are the same: **age regression** and the **television technique**. Age regression involves taking the participant back to the time when they witnessed the crime and asking them to re-live the experience. While this provides a firsthand account it may be distressing if the crime arouses emotionally painful memories. In the television technique, the participant is asked to witness the crime as though it was being played on a television. This method provides some emotional distance and can be less painful if memories contain disturbing content.

According to Gibson (1982) there have been some extravagant and unqualified claims about the power of forensic hypnosis. Most of these claims are not made on the basis of reliable scientific evidence, but by practitioners of hypnosis who stand to make financial gain from their claims. In contrast, scientific approaches to hypnosis attempt to make an informed judgement based on sound and reliable methodologies. There is considerable anecdotal evidence from case studies that hypnosis can improve eyewitness memories. In cases where serious crimes have been witnessed (armed robbery, rape, murder, etc.) and events have been 'repressed' because of emotionally painful content, there has been a return of these painful memories under hypnosis (Reiser 1990). Controlled laboratory studies, however, do not support these findings and suggest that memory of events under hypnosis is no better than under ordinary conditions. How can we explain the difference between the anecdotal case studies and controlled lab studies? Reiser (1990) suggests that the lab studies lack ecological validity and do not resemble real-life situations. For example, the lab studies do not use meaningful stimuli and so lack the level of emotional arousal present in real-life situations. Some recent studies that have attempted to improve the ecological validity of lab studies and make them more comparable to real-life situations have shown some support for the anecdotal case studies – that in fact hypnosis does improve recall.

Evaluation of forensic hypnosis

Gudjonsson (1992) identifies three potential problems with using forensic hypnosis. First, hypnosis may 'contaminate' memory. Information that occurs after an event has been encoded can be integrated into the memory representation of that event. Susceptible individuals under hypnosis may be more likely to alter their representations of that event and make more errors. Second, hypnotised witnesses are susceptible to leading questions and suggestions by the hypnotist, made unwittingly or not. After hypnosis, witnesses cannot differentiate between true recollection and suggestion. Finally, under hypnosis witnesses remember a great deal but also make many errors. However, they tend to show increased confidence in their fabricated memories. These problems are demonstrated quite clearly in a classic study by Putnam (1979; see also key research summary p. 169). Faced with the question of whether the advantages of forensic hypnosis outweigh the disadvantages it is fair to say that there are too many potential problems for memories produced under hypnosis to be considered as a reliable testimony. As Putnam (1979: 444) says:

> All of the effects seem to indicate quite clearly that under hypnosis, Ss [participants] answer more leading questions incorrectly and they are unaware that their responses are inaccurate.

However, this is not to say that forensic hypnosis has no value at all. Under hypnosis, witnesses may be able to access painful and emotional memories that would otherwise have remained repressed. This information could then be used as the basis for further police investigation.

Chapter summary

The detailed knowledge that cognitive psychologists have built up of the way people process information has made a valuable contribution to our understanding of the potential weaknesses of witness memory. The selective and biased way in which people encode information and the distortions produced by leading questions can result in testimony that is highly inaccurate. Witness memory is not an objective and accurate record of events but an interpretation of events subject to bias.

For example, attribution of blame or responsibility may be affected by attitudes (belief in a just world) or self-serving bias (the tendency to attribute failure to external factors). Some of the ways in which police attempt to identify suspects (e.g. ID parades) can result in mistaken identifications if guidelines based on psychological research are not followed. Similarly, attempts to construct a face from memory using photofit and identikit can be improved by starting with the face outline and hairline and by using cues. Some attempts to enhance the accuracy of witness testimony have produced promising results. Of particular interest are cognitive interview techniques, which, properly applied, produce testimony with more detail and fewer errors. The use of hypnosis raises several problems. In particular it may lead to more errors in testimony of which the witness is unaware. Its use should therefore be discouraged and evidence from hypnotic testimony is inadmissible in many courts of law.

Further reading

Ainsworth, P.B. (1998) *Psychology, Law and Eyewitness Testimony*. Chichester: Wiley. A very clear and accessible account of psychological research into eyewitness memory. Chapters 1–4 cover cognitive processes and eyewitness testimony, Chapter 7 covers the cognitive interview and Chapter 8 the use of hypnosis.

Kebbell, M. R. and Wagstaff, G.F. (1999) *Face Value? Evaluating the Accuracy of Eyewitness Information*. Police Research Series Paper 102. London: Home Office. A recently published summary of the conclusions drawn by psychologists on the issue of eyewitness memory.

http://www.a-levels.co.uk/science/psy.htm This A-Level website contains a Psychology section including a fantastic page called 'The Police Officer and Eyewitness Testimony' which is definitely worth a look.

8

The psychology of the courtroom

 Trial procedures
Jury processes
Child witnesses

This chapter examines courtroom processes and the ways in which psychology can help us to understand how juries reach their decisions. First, the two major types of trial procedure are discussed. There follows a consideration of the factors that can be shown to influence jury decisions including the strategies used by lawyers presenting evidence and the characteristics of the jury and the defendant. Finally, the issue of child witnesses is discussed in the context of the reliability of the testimony they produce.

TRIAL PROCEDURES

Criminologists usually make a distinction between two different types of trial procedure, the **adversarial system** (used in the UK) and the **inquisitorial system** (used in France and some other continental countries). One way in which trial procedures differ between adversarial and inquisitive systems is in terms of the role played by the judge (Thibaut and Walker 1978). Table 8.1 summarises the main differences.

Table 8.1 Comparison of adversarial and inquisitorial trial procedures (Thibaut and Walker 1978)

Adversarial	Inquisitorial
Judge plays a passive role.	Judge plays an authoritarian role.
Development of issues is in the hands of the parties or their legal representatives.	Development of issues is in the hands of the judge.
Presentation of evidence is in the hands of the parties or their legal representatives.	Presentation of evidence is in the hands of the judge.
Decision is made by judge or jury.	Decision is made by judge or jury.

The adversarial system involves two opposing parties, the prosecution and the defence. The aim is to win one's case, regardless of the truth. Attempts are made to establish a preferred version of events through a persuasive presentation of the facts and discrediting witnesses and victims. The aim of the inquisitorial system is to discover the truth. A biased presentation of facts is strongly discouraged. In this system, the judge takes control of proceedings, examines witnesses, calls for evidence from police and determines the 'facts' of the case.

These differences beg the question of whether one system is preferable to the other. Laboratory studies have attempted to address this question by asking participants to play roles in mock trials using one system or the other (Thibaut and Walker 1978). Generally, the results tend to favour the adversarial system over the inquisitorial system: participants were more satisfied with verdicts, the procedure was considered fairer and bias in favour of one verdict was reduced. One problem with this interpretation is that the mock trial studies only considered civil disputes where the facts were not in question (Stephenson 1992). In contrast, in criminal trials the facts *themselves* are frequently disputed. Therefore, the findings of such lab studies may be limited in their application to all types of trial.

Progress exercise

For AS Psychology you will have learnt about many concepts from social psychology including such topics as conformity, obedience, group processes, leadership and prejudice. Juries are also social situations and these social factors will have an impact on how juries reach decisions. Take one concept you have studied in social psychology (e.g. conformity or obedience) and consider how jury decision-making could be affected by that concept.

Persuasion techniques

An important aspect of jury trials is how the prosecution and defence attempt to persuade the jury that they are presenting the correct version of events. This section will consider three different social-psychological approaches to persuasion. It should be appreciated that much of the research discussed here is not directly concerned with what goes on in the courtroom. However, it is interesting to consider the extent to which these processes do go on inside the courtroom.

The Yale Model of persuasion

Hovland and Yanis (1959) developed the classic model of persuasion, which has subsequently become known as the 'Yale Model'. They argue that, if a message is going to be persuasive, one must consider several factors in addition to the message itself. These include the person giving the message (the source), the recipient of the message, and the situation in which the message is given. In the 1950s and 1960s a number of experiments were carried out at Yale University to investigate which characteristics of these components (source, message, recipient and situation) were persuasive and which others were not (see Table 8.2).

The results of these experiments have been summarised by Gross (1996). A message will be more persuasive if the source is charming, attractive, a knowledgeable expert (although this effect decreases with time – the 'sleeper effect') and is perceived as trustworthy (i.e. has no apparent ulterior motive). Factors which increase the persuasiveness of the message itself include *some* measure of emotional appeal (messages which provoke extreme emotions are less persuasive) and

Table 8.2 Summary of the Yale model of persuasion (Hovland and Yanis 1959)

Source	Message	Recipient	Situation
• Credibility	• Emotional appeal	• Resistance to persuasion	• Formal vs informal
• Attractiveness	• One sided vs two sided	• Level of education	
• Trust-worthiness	• Order of presentation		

presenting the most important information first (later information is more easily forgotten – known as the **primacy effect**). Additionally, a two-sided message should be used with recipients of a higher level of education and a one-sided message with recipients of a lower level of education.

A message is more persuasive when it is presented in an informal rather than a formal situation. A message is less persuasive when the recipient has a high level of resistance to persuasion. Finally, resistance to persuasion is high when counter arguments are available, when recipients are aware that someone is trying to persuade them and when recipients are well informed about a topic.

Story-telling in court

Social psychologists have noted that in order to 'make sense' of the world, people often fit the events around them into a story. Pennington and Hastie (1993) suggest that jurors are no different in this respect and will construct a story in order to make sense of the evidence presented. Jurors will return the verdict that has the 'best fit' with their story. It appears that the types of 'stories' told by lawyers can influence the jury's verdict.

Two story-telling strategies have been investigated (Aronson et al. 1997). When using **story order**, lawyers present evidence in the sequence that events occurred. When using **witness order**, lawyers present witnesses in the sequence they believe is most likely to persuade the jury, although this may not be the sequence in which the actual events occurred. In this way, the lawyer can leave their 'best' witness until last to try to finish on a dramatic note. An important study by Pennington and Hastie (1988) attempted to discover which strategy is more effective, using a mock jury approach (see key research summary, p. 170). This study showed that 'story order' is more likely to persuade a jury than 'witness order'.

Rhetorical strategies

Rhetorical strategies refer to devices used by speakers and writers in order to persuade an audience. Atkinson (1984) highlights the use of two particularly effective strategies referred to as two-part contrasts and three-part lists. These devices can regularly be seen in adverts, newspapers and political speeches (see Figure 8.1).

As illustrated by these examples, the two-part contrast uses what Atkinson refers to as the 'puzzle solution format'. The first line is used to puzzle the recipients and the second line is used to deliver the solution. The three-part list is a way of summarising a message using only three items. As Atkinson notes, it is virtually impossible to test such devices out in experimental studies. It is possible however, to use real-life examples of persuasive speeches and writings to analyse

---

Two-part contrasts:
'Now you can afford to be **out** . . . when the call comes **in**' [emphasis added] (advertising an answering machine).
'The party which promised to tax you **LESS** . . . is taxing **MORE**' [emphasis in original] (*Daily Mirror* 11 March 1981).

Three-part lists [emphasis added]:
'A Mars a day helps you **work, rest** and **play**' (advertising Mars Bars).
'This party has demonstrated that we are a party united in **purpose, strategy** and **resolve**' (Margaret Thatcher, Conservative Party Conference 1980).

Figure 8.1 **Some examples of two-part contrasts and three-part lists (Atkinson 1984)**

why they are so successful. Atkinson suggests that the effectiveness of two-part contrasts stems from the speaker's (or writer's) ability to format rival positions in an economical way. They are a way of summarising and simplifying complicated arguments and ideas. The three-part list is effective because it is possible to summarise the gist of a message in a way that is both brief and complete. It is difficult for an audience to recognise the completion point of a long list; however, once a three-part list is begun, the audience can anticipate a completion point, which requires increased attentiveness. The speaker (or writer) can move progressively towards a point to give the impression that all possibilities are covered.

JURY PROCESSES

The more serious criminal trials in the UK are conducted using a jury, whose eventual task is to decide on the guilt or innocence of the defendant. This decision is based on the evidence presented by the prosecution and defence. The legal system operates on the assumption that juries are rational and unbiased in the way they deliberate over the evidence. Unfortunately, this assumption is probably not justified. This section examines a number of psychological processes that might bias or distort the decision a jury comes to.

Juries deliberate in secret and, in many countries, it is illegal to ask jurors about their decisions, either before or after the event. This makes jury decision making very difficult to study. One way to overcome this problem in psychological research is by setting up studies using mock juries. This has the advantage that processes in jury decision making can be revealed but the disadvantage that they may not be realistic. Participants may not act in the same way in a mock jury when they know that their decision will not actually decide someone's fate. Despite this limitation, psychologists have carried out extensive research to try to unravel the mysteries of jury decision making.

Jury selection

When considering the question of jury selection, two questions have to be answered: first, how many people should sit on a jury? Second, what kind of people should make up the jury?

The number of jurors

In the UK and US juries have traditionally used twelve members. A number of criminologists have questioned whether this is the ideal number of jurors. Some courts in the US have experimented with using five or six jurors giving the opportunity to investigate whether size of jury affects the decision-making process. Smaller numbers of jurors tend to reach decisions more quickly (Saks 1977). However it seems that they are also less likely to examine evidence in detail, more likely to side with the prosecution and are generally less representative of society (Hans and Vladmir 1986). Based on this evidence it would seem sensible to continue with a twelve-person jury.

Who should make up the jury?

In the UK anyone can be selected for jury service who is aged 18 or over and who has the right to vote, although there are some exceptions including courtroom staff and other personnel involved in the legal process. In the US unsuitable candidates are screened out using the following criteria:

- Knowledge of pre-trial publicity.
- Attitudes towards the offence.
- Personal acquaintance with anyone involved in the case.

Some US courts use a highly controversial procedure called 'scientific jury selection'. The idea is that psychologists use a systematic, empirical, unbiased selection procedure to identify unsuitable candidates. Sales and Hafemeister (1985) identify three areas that could be used to identify unsuitable individuals:

- Personality, particularly authoritarian beliefs.
- Assessment of anxiety through non-verbal behaviour.
- Demographic characteristics such as age, sex and education.

Another technique used is the **juror bias scale**, designed to measure the level of pre-trial bias in jurors on several scales including expectancy that the defendant is guilty and belief in conviction and punishment (Kassin and Wrightsman 1983). Mock jury studies have shown that the juror bias scale can reliably detect jurors who are biased towards the prosecution – that is, those more likely to reach a guilty verdict. Based on such a test, individuals who are extremely biased towards the prosecution can be excluded from juries.

There are several problems with this kind of selection. First, there is an ethical debate about the value of scientific selection. On the one hand, it may seem a good idea to try and have as balanced and fair a jury as possible. On the other hand there is an argument that this should be achieved by using a cross-section of people from all areas of society and not by excluding those with extreme attitudes. Second, there is the question of who selects the jury and screens out 'undesirable' individuals. It is probable that, whoever does the screening, the make-up of the jury will simply reflect the values of the person or persons responsible for selection.

Jury decision making

Jury decision-making processes can be divided into evidential (those to do with the actual evidence) and **extra-evidential** (factors which influence decision making other than the actual evidence presented in court). This section will consider several extra-evidential influences including group processes, pre-trial publicity, witness confidence and characteristics of the defendant.

Courtroom evidence

Juries tend to attach considerable importance to the testimony of eyewitnesses, even though psychological research has shown that eyewitness memory can be unreliable (see Chapter 7). Harrower (1996) suggests that jurors (and people generally) have an implicit belief that memory and perception are an accurate record of events whereas psychological research has shown memory to be an active and constructive process. Even a discredited witness has an influence on jury decision making, although less influence than an unchallenged witness.

While psychological research has highlighted how important eyewitness testimony is to jury decision making, jurors tend not to see themselves as being influenced (Visher 1987). Hollin (1989) suggests that jurors are not aware that their decision making is influenced by eyewitness testimony. If this is the case then one solution might be to use psychologists as 'expert witnesses' to explain to the jury the problems involved with eyewitness testimony.

Group processes in jury decision making

According to Hastie et al. (1983) jury decision making goes through three stages (see Table 8.3).

Decision-making processes in groups can be affected by group dynamics. Psychological research into social influence has identified some of these factors (see Table 8.4) which may be applied to the decision making of a jury.

The group processes identified in Table 8.4 cannot be studied in real juries for obvious reasons – so the extent to which they occur in real juries could be questioned. However, they have been well established in laboratory studies and a range of field settings and there is no compelling reason to believe that juries are completely exempt from them.

Pre-trial publicity

High-profile cases often attract considerable media attention. It has been questioned whether pre-trial publicity has affected jury decision

Table 8.3 Stages in jury decision making (Hastie et al. 1983)	
Orientation period	• relaxed and open discussion • set agenda • raise questions and explore facts • different opinions arise
Open confrontation	• fierce debate • focus on detail • explore different interpretations • pressure on minority to conform • support for group decision established
Reconciliation	• attempts to smooth over conflicts • tension released through humour

Table 8.4 Group processes which may affect jury decisions (Putwain and Sammons 2001)

Group process	What it involves	Possible outcome
Conformity	A person in the minority feels pressured to agree with the majority.	Sceptical jurors will not 'fight their corner' about the case if they are in the minority.
Leadership	The leader of a group has considerable influence over the behaviour of group members.	The jury foreperson will have undue influence over the verdict of the jury members.
Group polarisation	The view reached by a group tends to be more extreme than that reached by members individually.	When asked to make a recommendation (e.g. about compensation) the jury will be excessively punitive or lenient.

Source: Reproduced with permission from *A2 Psychology in a Week*
© 2001 Letts Educational.

making. Psychological research seems to suggest that it does. In a study by Padawer-Singer and Barton (1974), one group of participants was given newspaper cuttings about a defendant's criminal record and protracted confession. Another group of participants read newspaper stories that omitted the biased details. Both groups listened to tapes of the trial and were asked to reach a verdict. Results showed that 78 per cent of participants exposed to the adverse publicity delivered a guilty verdict whereas only 55 per cent of participants not exposed to the adverse publicity delivered a guilty verdict.

In another study, jurors were surveyed in a case where defendants were accused of distributing marijuana (Moran and Cutler 1991). Results showed that the more prior knowledge jurors had about the case, the more likely they were to return a guilty verdict. However, the jurors themselves believed that their knowledge of the crime did not affect their ability to make impartial judgements. To conclude, the opinions of jurors may be influenced by pre-trial publicity in newspapers, radio and TV news programmes, especially if the information concerns prior convictions and confessions. Is it possible to eliminate these effects? One solution is to select juries who have not been affected by publicity. Hollin (1989) suggests that this is not a practical solution especially as juries are supposed to be representative of the community as a whole.

Witness confidence

Penrod and Cutler (1987) found in a mock jury study that witness confidence was the most important factor in judging whether evidence was considered reliable or not. Witnesses who employ powerful speech, that is, those who speak clearly and without hesitation are seen as more convincing, competent, trustworthy, intelligent and truthful. This may not be a problem if confident witnesses are actually giving more reliable evidence than are unconfident witnesses but this is typically not the case (Wells and Murray 1984). Confidence is not a good predictor of whether evidence is reliable or not.

Defendant characteristics

In an ideal world, a jury would be made up of unbiased and unprejudiced people, intelligent enough to comprehend the evidence and with the necessary verbal and social skills to contribute to discussion. In the real world however, research has shown that jury verdicts are influenced by irrelevant aspects of the defendant such as age, gender and race (Hollin 1995). This section discusses how these defendant characteristics can affect jury decisions.

Attractiveness

Research has shown that, in general, physically attractive defendants are treated better than unattractive ones in gaining acquittal, lighter sentences and the sympathy of the jury. However, this is not the case if they used their attractiveness to aid their crime. One reason for this

Criminals:	unattractive
	low socio-economic status
	of 'dubious' moral character
Non-criminals:	attractive
	high socio-economic status
	of previous 'good' character

Figure 8.2 **Stereotypes of criminals and non-criminals (Dane and Wrightsman 1982)**

might be the stereotypes that people (jurors included) hold about the appearance of criminals and non-criminals (see Figure 8.2). Unattractive people are deemed more likely to be criminals and so receive harsher sentences whereas attractive people are seen as less likely to be criminals and so receive lighter sentences.

This fact is not lost on barristers who advise defendants to improve their appearance as much as possible. An example of the effect of physical attractiveness on jury decision making can be found in an important study by Castellow et al. (1990; see key research summary p. 171).

Gender

Cruse and Leigh (1987) asked participants to act as a jury in a mock trial where a relationship had ended because of physical assault. The defendant was alleged to have attacked the victim with a knife. One group of participants was told that 'Jack Bailey' was accused of knifing 'Lucy Hill': 43 per cent of jurors found him guilty. The other group was told that 'Lucy Hill' was accused of knifing 'Jack Bailey': 69 per cent of jurors found her guilty. How can we explain these differences? One interpretation is that the woman was more likely to be judged guilty because she violated her gender role (i.e. women do not physically assault people). As such she was more likely to be viewed in negative terms (and therefore more likely to be found guilty).

In the US, African-American defendants are more likely to be found guilty than white-American defendants are. They are also more likely to receive the death penalty. Baron and Byrne (1994) suggest three possible reasons for this:

- Racial bias by juries.
- African-Americans commit more crimes.
- White-Americans have greater disposable income and so have the means to pay for a better quality of legal representation.

Some evidence suggests that racial bias may play a role. Pfeiffer and Ogloff (1991) found that white university students rated black defendants more likely to be guilty than white defendants. This was most pronounced when the victim was white. The effect disappeared when participants were reminded that all elements of crime must be proved beyond reasonable doubt. A study by Gordon et al. (1988) suggests that this racial bias may be a result of stereotypes about the type of crimes that people commit. Participants were asked to consider two cases, one burglary and the other fraud, before sentencing the defendant. In each case, there were two defendants, one black and the other white. Results showed that the black defendant received a longer sentence for burglary and the white defendant received a longer sentence for fraud. A later study by Gordon (1990) revealed that the different sentences for the black and white defendants may have been the result of racial stereotypes about crime. Black people were seen as more likely to be responsible for burglary and white people were seen as more likely to be responsible for fraud.

Imagine that you have been called up for jury service (a realistic possibility if you are over 18 years old). Using your knowledge of persuasion techniques and decision making, what measures could be taken to remain unbiased and impartial? Draw up a list of the topics you have studied for social psychology and consider what impact they might have on jury decision making.

Progress exercise

CHILD WITNESSES

In Chapter 7, psychological research into eyewitness memory was reviewed but the special issue of child witnesses was not considered. Common sense might seem to suggest that children are more prone to fantasy and imagination than adults and hence make less reliable witnesses. However, psychological research suggests that this may not be the case. This section considers the nature of childhood memory and, in particular, whether child testimony is any less reliable than that of an adult.

Childhood memory

It is generally believed that children's memories are not as reliable as adults' memories. An example of how the testimony of a child witness is seen as less believable than an adult testimony can be seen in a study by Leippe et al. (1992). In the first phase of the study, three groups of participants: college students, children aged 5–6 years old and children aged 9–10 years old, were recruited to take part in a study on skin sensitivity. Midway through the procedure, a female entered the room, made an enquiry and left. Afterwards, participants were asked questions and their 'testimony' was videotaped from behind a two-way mirror. The participants were asked to:

- Describe what had happened.
- Describe the physical appearance of the experimenter and the intruder.
- Describe what they said.
- Identify the experimenter and intruder from a range of photographs.

In the second phase of the study, other college students were asked to rate each participant's testimony for believability. Results showed that believability was found to depend more on age and speaking style than on the accuracy of the testimony. Although the students could successfully distinguish between the accurate and inaccurate testimonies, the difference was small. Children were rated as less accurate and less believable than adults, even though they were equally accurate. Adults were rated as more believable if they appeared to be confident.

Why are children's memories seen as less reliable and believable? Some explanations focus on maturation, suggesting that brain areas responsible for memory have not yet fully developed. Other explanations focus on psychological processes and suggest that the child has not yet developed the necessary general knowledge schemas required to interpret and organise information. According to Davies (1991) children's memories will improve rapidly between the ages of 5–10 for the following reasons:

- Growth in general knowledge helps children to locate their experiences.
- Learning 'scripts' or typical sequences of action. This aids memory.
- Learning better strategies for encoding new information.

Because of this immaturity in memory, a child witness may require prompting or the use of cues to provide a coherent account. This can pose serious problems, as children may be particularly prone to suggestibility.

Problems with children's testimony

Ainsworth (1998) identifies three common assumptions about child memory:

- The cognitive abilities of children are less well developed than those of adults, so their memory capacities are inferior.
- Children are unable to distinguish between fantasy and reality, so their reports cannot be trusted.
- Children are highly suggestible, so their testimony may easily be influenced by leading questions.

There is no evidence to support the notion that children are any more prone to fantasy than adults. In fact, children can produce accurate statements of witnessed events, although typically in less detail than adults can. The amount of detail increases with age (Jones 1987). Because children produce less detailed accounts, they may be more susceptible to the effects of leading questions than adults. This may not be because children's memories are more prone to reconstruction but because of the influence of adult authority. Moston (1990b) has shown that when children are questioned repeatedly they change their accounts because they begin to believe their own are wrong.

Children aged 12 or over produce the same level of detail as an adult and are no more susceptible to leading questions than adults (Loftus et al. 1990). In conclusion, there is no reason to discriminate between reliable and unreliable witnesses on the basis of age (Gudjonsson 1992). One method to prevent potential memory errors is to use the cognitive interview (see Chapter 7). Geiselman et al. (1990) found that cognitive interviewing led to children producing more accurate accounts than standard interview procedures did. In cases of sexual abuse, the cognitive interview can be particularly helpful in preventing memory errors (see below).

Sexual abuse

The most problematic area where child witnesses are concerned is where there have been claims of sexual abuse (Gudjonsson 1992). Tully and Tam (1987) suggest that in such cases, police should use the 'special care questioning technique' as follows:

- Assess the suitability of the child for interview.
- Avoid the use of leading questions (see the cognitive interview – chapter 7).
- Careful examination of the child's account.

When examining a child's account, Jones and McGraw (1987) claim it is possible to distinguish between a false and a genuine account (see Figure 8.3).

If children are carefully and sensitively interviewed their testimony can be remarkably reliable and valuable (Jones 1988).

False	Genuine
Lack of detail	Use personal pronouns
Lack of emotion	Age-appropriate words
No account of coercion	

Figure 8.3 **Characteristics of genuine and false accounts of sexual abuse using child witnesses (Jones and McGraw 1987)**

Chapter summary

Psychological research has made a useful contribution to our understanding of what happens during a trial. Legal professionals may try various persuasion tactics in **adversarial** trials, where the aim is to win one's case. Research suggests that story order is more effective for both prosecution and defence than witness order. Jury decision making may be affected by the make-up of the jury itself, group processes, pre-trial publicity and a range of defendant characteristics. For example, jurors may draw on 'criminal' stereotypes when assessing a defendant's innocence or guilt. However, for legal reasons, jury research cannot use real juries or trials and therefore it is uncertain the extent to which processes affecting jury decision making actually apply under real-life trial conditions. Finally, research into child witnesses has indicated that they are capable of producing testimony that is far more accurate than most people assume. However, care should be exercised when questioning children as pressure from adults may cause them to alter their testimony.

Further reading

Ainsworth, P.B. (1998) *Psychology, Law and Eyewitness Testimony*. Chichester: Wiley. Chapter 7 provides an accessible and recent review of research into child witnesses.

Ainsworth, P.B. (2000) *Psychology and Crime: Myths and Reality*. Harlow: Pearson Education. An excellent review of jury decision making can be found in Chapter 7.

Hollin, C.R. (1989) *Psychology and Crime: An Introduction to Criminological Psychology*. London: Routledge. Although slightly dated, Chapter 7 provides detailed coverage of research on jury decision making.

9

Punishing, treating and preventing crime

Imprisonment
Non-custodial sentencing
Psychological treatment programmes
Crime prevention

An obvious question to ask about offenders is, how can they be prevented from reoffending? This chapter examines some of the ways in which the judicial system responds to offenders, starting with a discussion of imprisonment and then considering some of the alternatives to prison. Consideration is then given to a number of psychological 'treatments' for offending which are examined in terms of their effectiveness in preventing reoffending. Finally, some strategies for crime prevention are discussed.

IMPRISONMENT

One of the many ways in which a judicial system can respond to crime is by imprisoning the offender. Imprisonment, depending on the view one takes, can serve a number of possible functions including:

- Retribution: making the offender 'pay' for their offence by subjecting them to an adverse environment.

- Incapacitation: preventing the offender from reoffending.
- Deterrence: making potential offenders 'think twice' about committing an offence because of the consequences involved.
- Reform: altering the offender so that, on release, they do not reoffend.

The exact function of imprisonment which is most emphasised depends largely on a person's political outlook, with more conservative commentators emphasising retribution and the more liberal emphasising the potential of imprisonment to reform the offender. However it appears to be a common view – amongst politicians at least – that prison is a worthwhile and effective response to the more serious types of crime. However, the evidence on reoffending following imprisonment does not necessarily support this view.

Does prison work?

Many offenders commit further crimes almost immediately upon release from prison. Bottomley and Pease (1986) report that throughout the 1970s and into the 1980s the reconviction rate in the UK remained steady at around 60 per cent. Zamble (1990) estimates that the reconviction rate in Canada was between 40 and 50 per cent during the 70s and 80s. Amongst young males in the UK the reconviction rate is as high as 82 per cent (Home Office 1994). Given that many crimes do not result in a conviction, the reoffending rates may be higher than the reconviction rates suggest. These data do not support the notion that a prison term significantly reduces the chance of reoffending.

Some commentators take the opposing view and suggest that imprisonment may increase the probability of further criminal behaviour, as prison acts like a 'college of crime'. However, Walker and Farrington (1981) compared first offenders given probation or suspended sentences with those imprisoned or fined and found that the latter group were *less* likely to be reconvicted. It does not seem, then, that imprisonment necessarily increases the likelihood of later reoffending. However, it should be pointed out that different subgroups of prisoners may respond to imprisonment in different ways, some becoming more likely and some less likely to reoffend.

Nonetheless, it is a commonly held view that imprisonment *should* reduce reoffending. The reasoning behind this is that imprisonment is aversive and that this should motivate the offender to alter their behaviour to avoid it in future. There are a number of possible reasons why this is not actually the case. Some commentators suggest that prisons are 'too soft' and that an increase in the degree of unpleasantness of the prison environment would act to reduce reoffending. This myth is easily dispelled because the aversiveness of the prison environment (as measured by, for example, degree of overcrowding) does not seem to affect reoffending rates. In fact, offenders who are released from overcrowded institutions appear to be more likely to reoffend than those who have served their sentence in less crowded prisons (Farrington and Nutall 1980). In addition, imprisonment has a number of adverse psychological effects on inmates (see below) and it is probably not reasonable to suggest that prison is any kind of 'easy option'.

A more likely explanation of the failure of prison to reform offenders lies in a combination of several factors. There is typically a long delay between an offence being committed and the offender being apprehended, brought to trial and subsequently imprisoned. Additionally, an offender may have acquired a number of immediate benefits from their crime, such as an increase in material wealth. Therefore, the short-term gains of crime may outweigh the more long-term negative consequences. This being the case, those who engage in criminal activities may come to see imprisonment as simply an occupational hazard of their criminal career. If apprehended and imprisoned, the only 'lesson' they learn may be that being caught (rather than committing crimes) leads to aversive consequences. Their behaviour may be modified by the experience of imprisonment but only insofar as they take steps to avoid being caught again (Ainsworth 2000).

Imprisonment is a common judicial response to violations of the law, but there is disagreement on what its purpose should be. Draw up a list of the possible functions of imprisonment. Do you think that imprisonment is an effective response to crime?

Progress exercise

Psychological effects of imprisonment

There is no doubt that imprisonment is an aversive experience and that prison, generally, offers an extremely unpleasant environment. Apart from the obvious problems of boredom and violence, there is some evidence that imprisonment can have a detrimental effect on prisoners' psychological functioning. A few studies have indicated that imprisonment can result in a psychotic reaction in some inmates. Heather (1977) tested a sample of prisoners in Scotland and found that 59 per cent of them reported significant psychological problems with 20 per cent reporting psychotic symptoms such as hallucinations and delusions. Rasch (1981) reported that about half of a sample of German inmates showed signs of psychological disturbance although none of them reported psychotic symptoms. A more consistent finding has been that inmates show higher levels of anxiety and depression than the general population. Longitudinal studies, such as that by Zamble and Porporino (1988), indicate that, early in their sentences, prisoners show high levels of anxiety and depression. These steadily decline over time, suggesting that anxiety, depression and hopelessness represent psychological responses to confinement which decline as the inmate adjusts to the situation.

Prisoners, compared to the general population, run an increased risk of suicide. Following the pattern observed with anxiety and depressive symptoms, this risk appears to be highest in the initial stages of imprisonment. According to Dooley (1990), the suicide rate in the British prison population is around four times that in the population at large. Those most at risk are those on remand awaiting trial and those serving life sentences, for which the period of greatest risk is the first year of confinement.

In general, then, the available data indicate that imprisonment has a detrimental effect on mental health. This is greatest at the start of the sentence and declines as the inmate adjusts to their circumstances and develops strategies for coping with incarceration. It is very likely that the characteristics of the individual prisoner influence how well they adjust to imprisonment. However, the data on which these observations are based are limited. Not many studies of the emotional well-being of prisoners have been conducted and in particular there has been a shortage of longitudinal studies (Blackburn 1993). Therefore, it may be unwise to make generalisations based on the studies described above.

NON-CUSTODIAL SENTENCING

Besides imprisonment, legal systems all over the world have a variety of other means of punishing and rehabilitating prisoners. Different countries favour different methods but in Britain and the US the commonest forms of non-custodial sentence are fines, probation and reparation (e.g. community service). There is evidence that, for some offenders, these forms of sentence are at least as effective as imprisonment and have a number of additional benefits. In particular, they are cheaper to administer than custodial sentences.

Fines

A fine is a sum of money paid to the authorities by an offender as restitution for an offence for which they have been convicted. The amount to be paid by the convicted person is usually set by the trial judge but must be within limits laid down by the law. Caldwell (1965) suggests that fines have a number of advantages over other forms of punishment. First, the system is economical as it costs little to administer, does not require outlay on the maintenance of the offender (unlike prison or probation) and provides a source of revenue for the state, country or city. Second, fines do not stigmatise the offender or expose them to the adverse effects of imprisonment and can be adjusted to reflect their financial circumstances. Third, fines can be imposed in situations where no other punishment is possible, for example, when a business, rather than an individual, is deemed to have broken the law. Feldman (1993) states that, for first offenders, fines are more effective than either imprisonment or probation in preventing reoffending. This is supported by Walker and Farrington (1981), who found that fines led to lower reoffending than probation or suspended prison sentences. There are, however, a number of arguments against the use of fines. First, the fine may be paid by the offender's family or friends, lessening its impact on the actual offender. Second, for many offences, such as prostitution and possession of drugs, fines are used in a routine way with no intention to reform the offender. Third, in some circumstances, fines can come to be seen as an 'operating cost' of offending. An example of this is the system of fines against companies that pollute the environment in the UK. Some companies have found that it is cheaper to pay fines and carry on offending than to make the necessary changes to ensure that pollution does not take place.

Probation

When an offender is placed on probation they are released into the community on the condition that they submit to the supervision and guidance of a probation officer, with whom they are expected to meet regularly. Typically, the offender is given a suspended prison sentence and is under threat of imprisonment if they fail to comply with the probation order. Probation may be used as an alternative to a custodial sentence but can also apply to offenders released from prison who may be expected to undergo a period of probation before being entirely discharged from the penal system. Probation has a number of obvious advantages over imprisonment. As with fines, the offender remains in the community, meaning that they are not stigmatised or exposed to the adverse effects of the prison environment. Additionally, probation is less costly to the authorities than imprisonment. According to Home Office figures for 1995, probation at that point cost around £105 per month compared to over £2000 per month for imprisonment. Although the actual cost of probation is probably underestimated in these figures, it is unlikely that the total cost of probation exceeds more than a tenth of that of imprisonment.

Many writers suggest that probation is less effective than imprisonment in preventing reoffending. However, recent data from the UK do not necessarily support this view. A study of 857 offenders in Kent found that 63 per cent of those imprisoned had reoffended within five years. By contrast, of offenders assigned to probation with a requirement to attend a group work programme, only 41 per cent had reoffended in the same time span (Oldfield 1996). However, this study also highlighted the fact that the content of a probation programme is a key factor in its effectiveness: for offenders sentenced to probation with the requirement to attend a day centre, reconviction rates were the same as for imprisonment at 63 per cent. Similar findings are reported by Roshier (1995) for a two-year comparative study run in Cleveland along the same lines as the Kent study. It was found that 64 per cent of imprisoned offenders reoffended within two years, compared with 41 per cent of offenders sentenced to probation. However, the Cleveland study also included offenders sentenced to community service and found that this was slightly superior to probation with only 37 per cent of offenders reoffending after two years. Glaser (1983), reviewing a number of studies, concludes that for the majority of offenders probation is as likely to prevent reoffending as is a custodial sentence. This is particularly the case for first offenders, for whom probation has the added advantage of avoiding the potentially 'criminalising' influence of imprisonment.

Notwithstanding the above findings, it is clear that probation will only be an effective rehabilitative measure if it is implemented in the correct way. Oldfield's (1996) study showed that the content of a probation programme significantly affected its chances of success. Additionally, research generally indicates that probation orders are far more likely to be effective in preventing reoffending if they are tailored to the characteristics of the individual offender. Of course, this requires adequate provision of personnel and resources: a shortage of suitably trained probation staff may mean that professionals within the probation service become so overloaded that they are unable to provide any effective support and guidance to the offenders for whom they are responsible.

Reparation and restitution

In a reparation-based punishment, such as community service, the offender is required to undertake a specified amount of work deemed to be of benefit to the community, such as maintaining cemeteries and repairing public buildings. Reparation is thus made to society, rather than to the offender's specific victim(s). By contrast, a restitution-based sentence requires the offender to compensate their victim(s) directly. In the US, both reparation and restitution have increased in popularity since their introduction (Evans and Koederitz 1983). By contrast, Blackburn (1993) states that they have been relatively little used in the UK. Schneider (1986) examined the effectiveness of restitution schemes in four different US communities. Young offenders were randomly allocated to either restitution or another type of sentence and followed up over three years. It was found that restitution was superior overall to more traditional punishments in preventing reoffending. However, the difference was only slight and there were large variations between programmes, with some being less effective than custodial sentencing, depending on the nature of the community and the way the programme was managed. From the offender's point of view, paying restitution to the victim may be equivalent to paying a fine and may suffer from the same drawbacks (see above). Feldman (1993) concedes that the fact that it is the victim and not the state who is paid may make a difference to some offenders. However, he points out that there appears to have been no research to investigate whether this is the case.

PSYCHOLOGICAL TEATMENT PROGRAMMES

The custodial and non-custodial measures described above are employed by the judicial system in its dealings with offenders. As such, they are designed to serve a number of purposes of which rehabilitation is only one. The apparent failure of judicial sanctions to make a significant difference to crime rates (Lipsey 1992) has prompted a number of psychologists to put forward rehabilitation programmes based on psychological principles. These differ from judicial sanctions in two important ways. First, their aim is solely to reduce the probability of reoffending, rather than exacting justice on the offender. Second, they are based on psychological theories of offending, rather than the (sometimes rather vague) notions of 'human nature' on which judicial sanctions often seem to be based. Although a large number of interventions have been tried, based on a wide range of theories, this section will concentrate on a small number of behavioural and **cognitive behavioural** treatments for offending: token economies, social skills training and **anger management**.

Token economies

A **token economy** is a treatment programme based on the principles of operant conditioning. The essential idea is that criminal behaviour is learned in the same way as any other behaviour (i.e. through reinforcement and punishment) and hence can be 'unlearned' and more acceptable behaviour learned in its place. Although token economies were initially developed for use with patients with mental health problems, they began to be applied to offenders in the mid-1960s and gained in popularity until the 1980s, by which time they were widely used in the US. In the UK, they have been applied in a more limited way (Yule and Brown 1987). Token economies must be implemented within an institution, typically a prison or facility for young offenders. The institution management draws up a list of desirable behaviours. These might include complying with rules, completing chores and interacting in a positive way. When an offender behaves as desired they are given a token. Tokens may subsequently be exchanged for reinforcers such as sweets, drinks and visits home. The rationale behind token economies is that, through selective reinforcement, socially approved behaviours are learned. At the same time, undesirable behaviours are extinguished through lack of reinforcement. The controlled environment of an institution allows reinforcement to be manipulated far more precisely than in other settings.

Initially, researchers were optimistic about the rehabilitative potential of token economies. Many studies have shown that the introduction of a token economy in an institution is followed by an increase in the targeted behaviours. For example, Hobbs and Holt (1976) report improvements in the behaviour of young male offenders and Ayllon and Milan (1979) report similar findings with adult prisoners. Unfortunately, evidence that token economies produce lasting benefits is much weaker. As was found with token economies in therapeutic settings, once reinforcement is discontinued (i.e. when the person leaves the institution) the behaviours previously reinforced tend to disappear. However, there is some evidence that token economies may be successful insofar as offenders who have been on such programmes return to crime more slowly that those who have not. For example, Cohen and Filipcjak (1971) found that, compared to an untreated control group, boys who had been in a token economy programme were less likely to have reoffended after one and two years. However, after three years reoffending rates in the two groups were the same. In general, token economies seem to be most effective at making offenders more manageable within an institution and Blackburn (1993) concludes that they have little real rehabilitative value. In addition to this, they raise a number of ethical issues. Concerns about the human rights implications of token economies have led to the closure of at least one such programme in the US (Nietzel 1979). One major ethical problem is that access to things like food and drink must be restricted if they are to have value as reinforcers. Many commentators suggest that access to such basic goods should be regarded as a right, not a privilege contingent on behaving in a particular way.

Social skills training

Social skills training (SST) is a cognitive behavioural treatment based on the assumption that offending – particularly violent offending – is related to deficits in social skills. That is, many violent offenders behave aggressively because they lack other, more appropriate means of dealing with interpersonal conflict. The rationale is that by training offenders in the social skills necessary to effective interaction they may be less likely to reoffend. There is no universally accepted list of skills that should be targeted in SST. A typical programme might concentrate on 'micro-skills' such as appropriate eye contact and distance during social exchanges (Feldman 1993) as well as more general ('macro') skills such as assertiveness and negotiation (Blackburn 1993). The techniques of SST vary from programme to programme but generally involve modelling (the observation and imitation of others) and role play alongside instruction in skills and feedback on performance from skills trainers.

An evaluation of SST as a treatment for offending must seek to answer three important questions. First, does SST lead to an improvement in the skills targeted; second, does this improvement generalise beyond the training situation to the offender's everyday interactions and, finally, does SST lead to a reduced risk of reoffending? As regards the first question, there is a range of evidence which suggests that SST does lead to improvements in targeted social skills (Goldstein 1986). For example, Spence and Marzillier (1981) report improvements in a range of micro-skills such as eye contact, head movement and speech content following SST. What is less clear is whether these improvements remain in the long term. Spence and Marzillier found that the improvements were present after three months but had disappeared after six months. Regarding the generalisation of skills learned during SST the evidence is mixed. Goldstein et al. (1989) report that, on average, only 15–20 per cent of offenders who had completed SST programmes generalised their skills to other situations. However, self-report data from trainees are more promising, with many reporting fewer social problems after training (Blackburn 1993). In terms of its effect on reoffending, SST does not seem to be significantly more effective than other interventions. Sarason (1978) reports the results of a study comparing SST with a discussion-based programme. The SST treatment concentrated on imparting skills to deal with problems which might arise on release from prison, whilst the discussion pro-gramme involved guided discussion of the same issues but with no formal training. Both were compared with a control group who received no treatment. SST was superior to no treatment: 31 per cent of the control reoffended within five years, compared to 15 per cent of the SST group. However, the discussion-based intervention was just as effective as SST, suggesting that the benefits apparent in both groups were the result of the additional attention arising from being on a treatment programme. However, one area in which SST may prove effective is in crime prevention. Aiken et al. (1977) suggest that SST can be used to equip adolescents with the social skills to resist peer pressure, which lessens the probability that they will become involved in criminal activities.

Anger management

Anger management refers to a set of cognitive behavioural techniques that aim to improve offenders' ability to deal effectively with feelings of anger. It is based mainly on the work of Novaco (1975) who suggested that many violent offenders become aggressive because they cannot deal effectively with anger, which they tend to displace on to inappropriate targets simply because they are available. Novaco stresses that the aim of anger reduction should not be to stop the offender from experiencing anger but rather to enable them to deal with their angry reactions more effectively. This involves imparting skills concerning self-monitoring, self-control and conflict resolution. According to Ainsworth (2000), anger reduction programmes are usually conducted in groups and involve three distinct stages: cognitive preparation, skill acquisition and application practice.

In the cognitive preparation stage, offenders are encouraged to analyse their own patterns of anger and to identify the kinds of situa-tions that would provoke an angry reaction from them. Following on from this, they attempt to analyse their thinking processes during angry outbursts and to recognise possible irrational thoughts that lead to aggressive responses. In the skill acquisition stage, offenders are trained in the skills that might help them to either avoid anger-provoking situations or deal with them more effectively. Skills that might typically be imparted include relaxation to avoid excessive arousal levels, assertiveness to help the individual make their point in an effective but non-aggressive way and other social and communication skills such as conflict resolution. Finally, in the application practice phase of the treatment, offenders are given opportunities to apply their new skills in a controlled and non-threatening environment. This involves role play, in which individuals act out scenarios based on situations that might previously have made them angry, using their new skills to deal with the situation more effectively. During this phase of the treatment, they receive extensive feedback on their performance from the therapist/counsellor and from other group members.

A number of studies have confirmed the effectiveness of anger management in a variety of situations including marital conflict. However, relatively few direct studies of anger management with offenders have been conducted (Blackburn 1993). Some of those that have been carried out have produced promising results. For example, Feindler et al. (1984) found that anger management in a group of young offenders produced improvements in problem solving and self-control and a reduction in aggressive behaviour. Ainsworth (2000) concludes that anger management is an effective way of reducing aggressive behaviour in offender populations. However, he adds that anger management programmes are likely to be successful only if they are well managed, given sufficient resources and the right individuals are assigned to them. The main problem with anger management programmes is that their long-term effectiveness with violent offenders has not yet been established (Blackburn 1993). Additionally, there are few data available on how well anger management compares with other forms of treatment. A study by Moon and Eisler (1983) suggests that training in assertiveness and problem solving may bring more benefits than the anger management programme put forward by Novaco.

CRIME PREVENTION

All of the measures reviewed above, both judicial and psychological, are forms of crime prevention insofar as they aim to prevent offenders from committing further crimes. However, this is only one possible approach to preventing crime and is not what is usually meant by 'crime prevention'. Brantingham and Faust (1976) make a useful distinction between primary, secondary and tertiary crime prevention.

- Primary prevention refers to reducing opportunities for crime without reference to the individuals who commit it.
- Secondary prevention refers to measures directed at those at risk of becoming involved in crime to prevent them from doing so.
- Tertiary prevention refers to preventing further criminal behaviour by those who have already offended. Measures such as anger management are an example of tertiary prevention.

The following section will focus on primary prevention. This type of crime prevention strategy emphasises the removal of opportunities for crime to occur, for example, by making it more difficult for criminals to steal property by fitting more secure door and window locks (known as 'target hardening'). Three other approaches that have proven popular – and at times controversial – in primary crime prevention are closed circuit television (CCTV) surveillance, defensible space and 'zero tolerance'. The first two of these are regarded as environmental approaches to crime prevention as they involve altering aspects of the environment in order to reduce the probability of offending.

CCTV surveillance

CCTV surveillance involves the placing of television cameras in potential crime locations through which activity can be monitored on remote screens. The purpose of CCTV is primarily to discourage crime by making it more likely that the criminal will be apprehended. However, it has other important applications in helping to identify offenders and alerting police to incidents (e.g. fights) as they happen. CCTV schemes have proven extremely popular and now account for a substantial proportion of the British Home Office's crime prevention budget (Ainsworth 2000). Studies indicate that they have been quite successful in reducing crime (Horne 1996) although their use does raise a number of concerns. For example, CCTV images can often be of poor quality and hence of little value in identifying offenders. Additionally, some commentators view the proliferation of CCTV as encouraging invasion of privacy, and heralding the advent of a 'Big Brother' society. A further potential problem is that CCTV, rather than reducing crime, simply displaces it to another location where there is no surveillance. Burrows (1980) reports a study of the installation of CCTV in four London Underground stations in an attempt to reduce robbery and theft.

In the year following CCTV installation crime at the stations fell by 70 per cent. Across the Underground network as a whole crime fell by 38 per cent but in the fifteen stations closest to the four with CCTV the fall was only 25 per cent. These figures appear to indicate that, although CCTV resulted in a marked reduction in crime where it was actually installed, at least some of this crime was displaced on to the surrounding area, resulting in a smaller fall there than in the Underground as a whole. However, it is highly unlikely that every, or even most of the crimes prevented in one location are displaced to another. Therefore it can be argued that CCTV surveillance is worthwhile as it prevents at least some crimes from being committed (Ainsworth 2000).

Defensible space

An alternative approach to environmental crime prevention is derived from Newman's (1973) concept of **defensible space**. Defensible spaces are the areas of residential locations which are recognised as 'belonging to someone' and which fall under high levels of natural surveillance (e.g. from passers by or from windows in dwellings from which residents look out). Newman suggested that defensible space heightened feelings of territoriality (i.e. protection of your own space) amongst residents and consequently deterred crime. Newman presented data that purported to show that there were fewer robberies in locations with good defensible space properties. Additional support for the defensible space theory comes from a study by Wilson (1980) in which vandalism on a London housing estate was investigated. As defensible space theory predicts, vandalism was heaviest on the ground floor, near entrances, in underground garages and in areas that were used as routes to other locations.

However, the defensible space theory has been extensively criticised. Feldman (1993) suggests that Newman's original data show a far closer relationship between robberies and the number of local families receiving welfare benefits than the physical characteristics of the buildings. In the study by Wilson cited above, the best predictor of the degree of vandalism was the number of children living in the block, rather than the defensible space properties of the buildings. However, research by Taylor et al. (1980) found a small association between defensible space and crime rates. Taylor et al. revised Newman's theory to include a range of other variables. These include 'signs of defence' (physical or symbolic barriers against access by outsiders), 'signs of appropriation' (indications that an area is used and cared for) and the strength of local networks of communication. In their model, these variables interact to increase or decrease the crime rate in a particular location. In conclusion, it is fair to say that altering the physical environment can have the effect of reducing crime but that defensible space plays a relatively minor role in offending. Consequently, its role in crime prevention is likely to be limited.

> Imagine that you have been asked to advise a Local Residents' Association on crime prevention in their area. Which recommendations would you make?

Progress exercise

Zero tolerance

The term **zero tolerance** refers to a policing strategy in which law enforcement agencies respond vigorously to all criminal offences that occur in an area. This not only means thorough investigation of serious offences but also 'cracking down' on apparently trivial ones such as minor acts of vandalism. Zero tolerance originated with the work of Wilson and Kelling (1982) who put forward a set of ideas that have become known as the 'broken windows' theory. They argued that areas in which petty crime appears not to be policed 'invite' more serious offenders to increase their activity. The reason for this is that such areas convey the impression that serious crime is unlikely to be investigated. Wilson and Kelling identified two sets of factors that are important in conveying this impression: physical and behavioural. Physical manifestations of disorder include graffiti, litter and vandalism (e.g. broken windows). Behavioural factors include minor 'nuisance' offences such as public urination and soliciting by prostitutes. Translated into a policing strategy, the broken windows theory suggests that police should concentrate on reducing 'quality of life' crimes like vandalism and public urination by arresting and charging those found committing such offences, a relatively heavy-handed response. It follows that physical and behavioural manifestations of disorder will be reduced and, hence, so will the incidence of more serious offending.

The most famous example of the implementation of a zero tolerance policing strategy is New York City, where it was introduced in the early 1990s. Over the course of this decade, there was a significant reduction in crime, including serious crime. Other cities that implemented zero tolerance reported similarly impressive results. For example, the Indiana Police Department found that increasing traffic enforcement in targeted areas significantly reduced the number of robberies (Sherman 1997). Over the same period, there was a sharp decline in violent and property crime across the US as a whole.

These results appear to support the idea that zero tolerance significantly cuts crime. The question is, does this happen for the reasons suggested by Wilson and Kelling? Research suggests that this is only one contributing factor. Kelling and Coles (1996) report that, in New York, many of those arrested for minor offences had a criminal record for more serious offending. This may mean that their arrest, by removing them from circulation, prevented them from committing serious crimes. Kelling and Coles also report that zero tolerance arrest strategies discouraged offenders from carrying firearms, which had a major impact on armed robberies and murders. Finally, the general decline in crime in the US was the result of a great many factors including a growing economy, a decline in the use of crack cocaine and increased gun control in metropolitan areas (Grabowski 1999). William Bratton, the police commissioner who introduced zero tolerance to New York, agrees that enforcing the law for petty offences was not the only factor that led to the dramatic fall in crime. He also cites improved intelligence about criminal activity and increased accountability for police precinct commanders as improving the overall quality of policing in New York (Bratton 1998).

Zero tolerance is therefore not necessarily the quick-fix solution to crime that has been claimed and there is some evidence that suggests it can be counterproductive. For example, a number of US cities introduced curfews for young people in the mid-1990s in order to cut the rate of juvenile offending. An analysis of crime statistics in cities with and without curfews by Males and Macallair (1998) indicated that they did not affect juvenile crime or juvenile violent death rates.

Comparing San Francisco (no curfew) with San Jose (curfew vigorously enforced) they found that whereas violent crime, juvenile homicide and juvenile violent death all decreased in San Francisco, violent crime actually increased in San Jose. Males and Macallair concluded that the only effect of youth curfews was to remove law-abiding young people from the streets, leaving them emptier and hence more conducive to crime.

To conclude, zero tolerance policing can have the effect of reducing crime but it is not a universal cure for crime. It is likely to be successful only as part of a larger package of measures aimed at improving the effectiveness of policing in a particular locality. Its implementation must be carefully considered, as it is not appropriate for all areas. In particular, there is the danger that zero tolerance may lead to increased targeting of ethnic minorities, leading to alienation, reduced co-operation with the police and the possibility of urban disturbances (Harrower 1998).

Chapter summary

This chapter has shown that the utility of judicial measures in preventing reoffending is limited. In particular, for most offenders, imprisonment seems to be no more effective than non-custodial sentencing, which may be seen as preferable, as it is cheaper for the authorities and less detrimental to the offender. Limited success has been achieved with psychological interventions for offending, with cognitive-behavioural techniques appearing more effective than purely behavioural ones. Finally, there is a range of crime-prevention strategies that appear to reduce the incidence of offending in particular locations. These include CCTV monitoring and defensible space. Evidence suggests that such measures can have the effect of decreasing crime in a particular area although there remains the possibility that at least some of this crime is simply displaced to other areas. Zero tolerance refers to the rigorous enforcement of the law, even for minor offences. The evidence suggests that this may lead to a reduction in crime but only if used in conjunction with other measures to improve the quality of policing in a given area. Whilst all of these measures have some impact on the crime rate, none of them can justifiably be called a solution to the problem of crime.

Further reading

P.B.Ainsworth (2000) *Psychology and Crime: Myths and Reality.* Harlow: Pearson Education. Chapter 8 contains detailed coverage of imprisonment and treatments for offenders.

10

Study aids

 Improving your essay writing skills
Key research summaries

IMPROVING YOUR ESSAY WRITING SKILLS

At this point in the book you have acquired the knowledge necessary to tackle the exam itself. Answering exam questions is a skill that this chapter shows you how to improve. Examiners obviously have first-hand knowledge about what goes wrong in exams. For example, candidates frequently do not answer the question which has been set, rather they answer the one they hoped would come up. Or they do not make effective use of the knowledge they have but just 'dump their psychology' on the page and hope the examiner will sort it out for them. A grade 'C' answer usually contains appropriate material but tends to be limited in detail and commentary. To lift such an answer to a grade 'A' or 'B' may require no more than a little more detail, better use of material and coherent organisation. It is important to appreciate it may not involve writing at any greater length, but rather necessitate the elimination of passages which do not add to the quality of the answer and some elaboration of those which do.

The essays given here are notionally written by an 18 year old in thirty minutes and marked bearing that in mind. It is important when writing to such a tight time limit that you make every sentence count. Each essay in this chapter is followed by detailed comments about its strengths and weaknesses. The most common problems to watch out for are:

- Failure to answer the question set and instead reproducing a model answer to a similar question which you have pre-learned.
- Not delivering the right balance between description and evaluation/analysis.
- Writing 'everything you know' about a topic in the hope that something will get credit and the examiner will sort your work out for you. Remember that excellence demands selectivity, so improvements can often be made by removing material that is irrelevant to the question set and elaborating material which is relevant.
- Failing to use your material effectively. It is not enough to place the information on the page, you must also show the examiner that you are using it to make a particular point.

Question One: OCR Specimen Question 2000

Section A

Answer **one** question from this section.
1. (a) Describe **one** laboratory study of eyewitness testimony.
   [6 marks]
   (b) Compare and contrast the laboratory method to study eyewitness testimony with one alternative method.
   [10 marks]
2. (a) Describe **one** study which demonstrates the development of moral and legal judgement in children.
   [6 marks]
   (b) Discuss the use of children in psychological studies of crime.
   [10 marks]

Section B

Answer **one** question from this section.
3. (a) Describe the jury decision-making process.
   [10 marks]

(b) Discuss jury decision-making processes.
  [16 marks]

(c) If you were a member of a jury, suggest what rules you may make for yourself to prevent you from making the wrong decision. Give reasons for your answer.
  [8 marks]

4. (a) Consider psychological studies of offender profiling.
  [10 marks]

(b) Evaluate psychological studies of offender profiling.
  [16 marks]

(c) Suggest what the aims of profiling should be. Give reasons for your answer.
  [8 marks]

Answer to question one, with examiner's comments

1(a) One classic lab study into eyewitness memory was carried out by Loftus and Zanni (1975). Participants watched a film of a multiple car crash and answered a questionnaire about the film afterwards. On the questionnaire were six critical questions. Half of the participants were given questions like: 'Did you see *a* broken headlight?' and the other participants were given questions like: 'Did you see *the* broken headlight?' Results showed that 7 per cent of participants replied yes when asked if there was *a* broken headlight and 15 per cent of participants replied yes when asked if they saw *the* broken headlight, even though there was no broken headlight in the film. **Mark: 5/6**

Examiner's comment

The answer gives a clear and concise account of one laboratory study. It is well expressed and contains a lot of accurate detail. It might have included the conclusions that can be drawn from this study.

1(b) One alternative methodology to using lab-based studies is to use field-based studies. A field-based study is one which takes place outside of the lab and in the 'real world'. In general, lab studies have the advantage that they control for potential threats to internal validity and so a causal relationship can be established. However, lab studies like Loftus and Zanni's described above may not be generalisable to real-world settings. In a lab study, participants are not subjected to the kind of stress present in a real crime. In contrast, findings from field studies have high ecological validity and can be generalised to other contexts. However, field studies may not control for potential threats to internal validity and so results may have been affected by a number of confounding variables. As a result it may be harder to establish cause and effect relationships. **Mark: 7/10**

Examiner's comment

This is a thoughtful and appropriate answer. The answer identifies an alternative method and makes some points of comparison and contrast. It is true that laboratory studies offer greater opportunity for control of the situation and, often, the participants. I'm not sure, however, what is meant by 'internal validity' and although it sounds good (and is therefore an example of good bluffing), it does not add much to the answer. The answer seems to assume that any field study should also be a study of a criminal event, and this is not necessarily the case. It would be possible to stage a range of events for people to witness that did not cause offence or stress. The point about ecological validity is well made, although it might have been useful to add an example of one of the features that enhances this type of validity. It is also correct to note that causal relationships are easier to establish in controlled conditions. Overall, this answer contains a lot of good points in a relatively small space, though there are more points of contrast than comparison.

Q1   Total = 12/16

4(a)   Ressler et al. (1988) describes how the FBI carried out interviews with thirty-six serial murderers in 1979. Results from these interviews suggested two types of murderers: organised and disorganised. Organised murders are planned, the victim is usually a targeted stranger and few clues are left. This type of murderer is of above average IQ, sexually and socially competent and living with their partner. The disorganised murder is unplanned, sudden and there is little attempt to hide evidence. This type of murderer lives alone and is socially and sexually inadequate. Canter and Heritage (1990) analysed twenty-seven rapists to see if the interaction between offender and victim mirrored interaction in other areas of the rapist's life. They suggested that a rapist who initiated little sexual contact would be living alone; an offender using degrading language would have difficult relationships with women at home and work; and the offender who destroys evidence has a previous criminal record. **Mark 6/10**

The answer outlines two studies of offender profiling. The outlines are well expressed and contain a reasonable amount of detail. It would have been helpful to start the answer with a brief description of what we mean by offender profiling and then use the studies to illustrate this process. It is a controversial technique and relies on the idea that we can create effective typologies of people that can be used to predict behaviour. The answer is a little brief and for full marks should have outlined one or two more studies.

4(b) The FBI approach has been used successfully to solve murders. Evidence from the crime scene is sent to the FBI, who find matches to previous murders and profile the likely characteristics of the murderer. This approach has been criticised by Canter as no more scientific than astrology and because the original study was flawed because it was based on interviews with disturbed and manipulative individuals. Canter believes that his approach, to look for consistency between the crime and other areas of the offender's life, is much more scientific and based in psychological theory than the FBI approach. However there is no clear criteria for evaluating offender profiling and so it is difficult to judge whether a profile is successful or not. For example, if a profile is 50 per cent correct, is this a success or a failure? **Mark: 8/16**

Examiner's comment

The answer contains some appropriate evaluative points. It is fair to say that the bottom line for offender profiling is whether it helps to catch offenders. If it doesn't then it is pointless. Of course, it might be used to catch the wrong person, and the history of criminal investigations is full of incorrect lines of enquiry based on personal profiles. For example, the case of the Yorkshire Ripper was held back because the police erroneously believed the offender came from the North East of England. The answer could have raised some issues about the problems of typologies, and the problems of conducting research in this area. It is likely, for example, that criminals who fit the profile are more likely to be caught than criminals that do not. This will give an optimistic view of the effectiveness of the profiling process.

4(c) Offender profiling should aim to be an investigative tool, that is, it should help the police to apprehend the offender. If an offender profile does help the police in this way then it is not of much use. One way an offender profile could help an investigation to move forward is by narrowing down the list of suspects to those which fit the profile. This would enable police resources to be concentrated on a smaller number of potential suspects. Another way offender profiles could be useful is in predicting if the offender will strike again, and if so when and where. Such information could be used to apprehend an offender.
Mark: 7/8

Examiner's comment

The answer is a reasonable response to the question. There appears to be a typo in the second sentence (a missing 'not') but the examiners will go with the sense of the answer rather than the detail.
Q4   Total = 21/34

Question Two: Edexcel Specimen Question 2000

Topic B: Criminal Psychology

Answer all three questions

B1

> **Source One**
> The following statement was found in the local newspaper: 'It was only to be expected that Joe would start stealing cars. After all, everyone expected him to do it.'

(a) Outline what is meant by the self-fulfilling prophecy.
[4 marks]

(b) Evaluate the self-fulfilling prophecy as an explanation of anti-social behaviour.
[6 marks]

B2

Source Two

'Laboratory work . . . has indicated that the search for a plausible story is a powerful motive for individual jurors.'

Source: Hewstone, Stroebe and Stephensen (1996: 588)

The above quote considers the question: 'Do juries make good decisions?'

(a) Describe TWO influences on decision-making processes as they relate to a jury.
[6 marks]

(b) Evaluate ONE study in the area of jury decision-making.
[6 marks]

B3

Source Three

'There is evidence from crime figures that mugging, rape and violent crime are more common now than they were a few years ago. It is thus more important now than ever to find ways in which aggressive behaviour can be controlled and reduced. Psychologists have suggested a number of solutions.'

Source: Eysenck (1996: 106)

The above source suggests the importance of controlling aggression in treating crime.

(a) Describe TWO psychological means of controlling aggression that have been suggested by psychologists.
[6 marks]

(b) Evaluate the means of controlling aggression you have described in (a) above.
[8 marks]

Answer to question two, with examiner's comments

B1(a)   A self-fulfilling prophecy is basically when we live up to expectations because we believe them to be true. This can happen when someone is labelled as a 'bright' student and then they actually start to perform better. **Mark 2/4**

Examiner's comment

This answer is a brief definition. The question is worth 4 marks and so requires more detail than is provided here. For example, the answer could have included a research example to illustrate the process.

B1(b)   The idea that anti-social behaviour occurs as a result of a self-fulfilling prophecy is very hard to test. It would not be ethical to label someone as a 'criminal' just to see if they actually became a criminal. Because of this problem, there is a lack of experimental evidence. The self-fulfilling prophecy remains an interesting idea, but only with anecdotal evidence. **Mark 4/6**

Examiner's comment

This answer gives a detailed account of lack of direct evidence for the self-fulfilling prophecy as an explanation for anti-social behaviour. On its own this is not enough to gain full marks. A better answer would have considered more factors. For example, alternative explanations of anti-social behaviour.
B1   Total = 6/10

B2(a)   One psychological factor which can influence the decision-making process of jurors is group processes. If a juror is in a minority, they may conform to the majority view and not 'fight their corner'. The leader of the group, the jury foreperson, will have a larger influence than other group members. Finally, due to group polarisation, the jury may give a more lenient or harsh judgement than individual jurors would on their own. Another psychological factor is the characteristics of the defendant. Research has shown that jurors are influenced by stereotypes about gender, race and attractiveness of the defendant. **Mark: 5/6**

Examiner's comment

The question asks for two influences on jury decision-making for six marks, which is three marks for each. This answer is a bit lop-sided, in that there is much more material given for group processes than for characteristics of the defendant. A better answer would have contained more research on defendant characteristics, perhaps explaining how juror judgements are affected by stereotypes.

B2(b) A study by Castellow et al. (1990) showed that jurors make judgements about the character and personality of the defendant based on appearance. This study shows evidence that jury decisions are based in part on stereotypes and provides support for 'Scientific Jury Selection' to choose people who are the least biased and prejudiced. **Mark: 2/6**

Examiner's comment

On the plus side, the answer does say which study is being evaluated. Remember, the examiner does not know unless the answer makes it clear which study is being evaluated. On the down side the answer does not give very much information. A better answer would have explored more issues such as what types of stereotypes are held about defendants and the methodology used.

B2   Total = 7/12

B3(a) One psychological method for reducing aggression is social skills training. In social skills training the offender is taught non-aggressive responses to frustrating and difficult circumstances. These are practised in a role-play situation and feedback is given by their partner. Another method is cognitive-behaviour therapy. The offender is taught to identify how they think and feel in situations which make them angry. The aim of therapy is to change how they think and feel in such situations, so they do not respond with aggression. **Mark: 4/6**

Examiner's comment

The two methods for reducing aggression are described briefly, but lack detail. A better answer would have given more detail. For example, the types of social skills role-played or the type of dysfunctional beliefs which give rise to aggression in cognitive-behaviour therapy.

B3(b)   Social skills training has been shown to reduce aggressive behaviour, although there are questions over whether offenders can use the skills they learnt in training in other situations. More seriously, even if appropriate social skills are learnt, this may not reduce offending. Cognitive-behaviour therapy is also effective in reducing aggression. Meta-analytic outcome studies have found an effect size of approximately +0.6, a medium strength effect. **Mark: 4/8**

Examiner's comment

The two methods for reducing aggression are evaluated briefly, but also lack detail. A better answer would have given more evaluative points or explained the existing points in greater detail.
B3   Total = 8/14

Question Three: AQA-B Specimen Question 2000

Since the age of 14, Pete has been in trouble with the police. When he was 15 years old he received his first custodial sentence and was sent to a young offenders' institution after a number of burglaries. Now, at the age of 18, he has been sentenced to a term of imprisonment after being convicted for dealing in drugs. At his trial the judge commented: 'You have been given this sentence in an effort to deter you from a life of crime.'

(a) Describe the main features of **one** psychological technique used to treat Pete.
   [5 marks]
(b) Evaluate the effectiveness of imprisonment as a means of punishing offenders for their crimes. Refer to **at least three** empirical studies in your answer.
   [15 marks]

Answer to question three, with examiner's comments

(a) One technique used to treat Pete could be social skills training. This involves teaching Pete appropriate ways of behaving in social situations such as how to negotiate difficult situations and the right level of eye contact and interpersonal distance. These are practised in role-play situations and feedback given by trainers. Although Pete's social skills may improve, he might not stop dealing drugs. **Mark: 4/5**

Examiner's comment

This answer correctly identifies social skills training as a technique that could be used to treat Pete. Some accurate description of the technique is provided: appropriate behaviour in social situations, level of eye contact and interpersonal distance. The answer also correctly identifies the use of role-play and feedback that would be used with Pete. The final sentence in the answer, whilst interesting, is not relevant to the question set. To gain full marks some further detail of the technique would be required. This may be, for example, types of role-play, other non-verbal behaviour, importance of feedback.

(b) Bottomley and Pease (1986) reported that during the 1970s and 1980s, 60 per cent of offenders were likely to commit more crimes once they had been released from prison. This figure suggests that prison is not effective in punishing offenders. A 1994 Home Office report supports this finding, finding that up to 82 per cent of offenders will reoffend when they have been released from prison. One possible reason is that prison acts as a 'college of crime', where first-time offenders are surrounded by a culture where criminal behaviour is the norm. Support for this idea comes from study by Walker and Farrington (1981). They found that a group of first-time offenders who were given probation or fined were less likely to reoffend than a group given a prison sentence. **Mark: 8/15**

Examiner's comment

This answer refers to two empirical studies and a Home Office report, indicating that the candidate knows quite a bit of psychology in this area. The answer, in the second sentence, draws a general conclusion about the results of the study by Bottomley and Pease, thus demonstrating AO2 skills. The candidate uses the Home Office report to provide further support to this study, again demonstrating AO2 skills. The evaluation that prison may 'act as a college of crime' is insightful and again shows AO2 skills. This idea is then given empirical support by citing the Walker and Farrington study. The findings of this study are briefly described.

This question would gain 4 marks for AO1 and 4 marks for AO2. What is clearly missing from the answer is theories of why people are imprisoned – rehabilitation, punishment, public safety, making an example, etc. To gain higher marks the candidate might focus more clearly on imprisonment as a treatment and perhaps briefly outline the types of imprisonment available. More discussion of the effectiveness and consequences of imprisonment would also help to score higher marks. This could be done either through citing more studies and/or evaluation of the different theories of reasons for imprisoning people. Some evaluation of a study could also be provided. An average to good answer that could easily be improved on with use of theory and more studies.

Total for Question Three = 12/20

KEY RESEARCH SUMMARIES

Loftus, E.F. and Zanni, G. (1975) 'Eyewitness testimony: the influence of the wording of a question' *Bulletin of the Psychonomic Society*, **5(1), 86–88.**

AIM To investigate the effect of misleading questions on eyewitness memory.

METHOD One hundred participants watched a film of a multiple car accident and subsequently were asked to complete a twenty-two-item questionnaire containing six critical questions. For half of the participants, the critical question used the indefinite article (e.g. Did you see *a* broken headlight?). The question was changed to the definite article for the remaining half of participants (e.g. Did you see *the* broken headlight?).

RESULTS 7 per cent of participants given the indefinite article replied 'yes' whereas 15 per cent of participants given the definite article replied 'yes'. However, there was no broken headlight in the film.

IMPLICATIONS From one point of view, it could be argued that only 15 per cent of participants were deceived and since the majority were not then the effect of misleading questions is not a great one. However, there are several important points to be made. First, some participants were deceived in a relatively simple task and further research is required to ascertain exactly which conditions are required for leading questions to produce errors. It is possible that other conditions would produce much higher rates of error in eyewitness memory. Second, introducing misleading information in the question by simply asking participants whether there was a broken headlight (when there was none) was enough to produce memory distortion. Finally, the difference between the use of '*a*' and '*the*' in critical questions produced important results. *The* broken headlight implies there was a broken headlight whether the participant spotted it or not. Approximately twice as many participants made errors under this condition, showing how witnesses may be 'led' into giving certain responses to a question.

Putnam, W.H. (1979) 'Hypnosis and distortions in eye witness memory' *International Journal of Experimental and Clinical Hypnosis*, **27**, 437–448.

AIM To test the hypothesis that witnesses would make more errors when answering leading questions when hypnotised.

METHOD Participants were shown a video of an accident involving a car and a bicycle. The car turned in front of the bicycle resulting in a collision between the car and bicycle, throwing the rider to the floor. After watching the video, participants were told to imagine they had witnessed the accident and were to be questioned by the police. Participants were randomly allocated to one of two conditions. Half of the participants were tested in a normal waking state and half under hypnosis. From each condition, half of the participants were tested fifteen minutes after watching the video and the remainder twenty-four hours later. Participants were given a fifteen-item questionnaire to complete about the video. Six of the questions were leading questions.

Participants were also asked how certain they were of their response to each question from a scale of 1–5 (1 = guess and 5 = absolute certainty).

RESULTS On non-leading questions, there was no difference between the hypnotised and non-hypnotised participants: hypnosis did not improve recall. However on the leading questions, hypnotised participants made significantly more errors than those participants who were not hypnotised. Furthermore, the hypnotised participants were just as confident of their responses as the non-hypnotised participants.

IMPLICATIONS Whether these problems with hypnosis are actually a problem for the police depends on how hypnosis is used. As Gibson notes, it is the nature of police inquiries to generate as many potential leads as possible, which are subsequently investigated. If forensic hypnosis is used to generate leads that can then be checked out, then false material may not be a problem. If the memories produced under forensic hypnosis are regarded as an accurate testimony then false material can become a serious problem. In fact, under these conditions, the use of forensic hypnosis could be considered a fabrication of evidence.

Pennington, N. and Hastie, R. (1988) 'Explanation-based decision making: effects of memory structure on judgement' *Journal of Experimental Psychology: Learning, Memory and Cognition*, **14, 521–533.**

AIM To test the hypothesis that jurors are more easily persuaded by 'story order' (presenting evidence in the sequence that events occurred) than 'witness order' (presenting witnesses in the order most likely to persuade a jury).

METHOD Participants were asked to be jurors in a mock murder trial. The lawyers representing both the defence and the prosecution varied the order in which evidence was presented.

RESULTS The results provided support for the story order hypothesis.

Experimental condition	Defence	Prosecution	Guilty verdict
Group A	Story order	Story order	59 per cent
Group B	Witness order	Witness order	63 per cent
Group C	Story order	Witness order	31 per cent
Group D	Witness order	Story order	78 per cent

IMPLICATIONS From these results, it is clear that story order is more persuasive than witness order. It appears that it is easier for the jurors to construct a story out of events told in the correct order than when events are told in the wrong order to try to increase their impact. Pennington and Hastie (1990) suggest that the reason why 80 per cent of criminal court cases return guilty verdicts in the US is because prosecution lawyers tend to use story order and defence lawyers tend to use witness order. On the basis of the above study, all lawyers would be advised to use the story order strategy.

Castellow, W.A., Wuensch, K.L. and Moore, C.H. (1990) 'The effects of physical attractiveness of the plaintiff and defendant in sexual harassment judgements' *Journal of Social Behaviour and Personality*, **5,** 547–562.

AIM To test the hypothesis that juries make judgements about the personality and character of the defendant based on their appearance.

METHOD In the first phase of the experiment, participants (mock jurors) were asked to read the trial summary of a case in which a 23-year-old secretary-receptionist accused her male employer of sexual harassment. It was alleged that he repeatedly made sexual remarks, attempted to kiss and fondle her and described in detail sexual acts he would like to enjoy sharing with her. In the second phase of the experiment, participants were shown photographs of the defendant (the employer) and the plaintiff (the secretary) and asked to decide whether the defendant was guilty or innocent. Participants were shown one of four different combinations of photographs. In the first two combinations, the plaintiff and defendant were both attractive or both unattractive. The final two combinations involved an attractive plaintiff and an unattractive defendant and vice versa.

RESULTS The different photo combinations produced different results.

Photo combination	Percentage of mock jurors who found the defendant guilty
Attractive plaintiff and attractive defendant	71 per cent
Attractive plaintiff and unattractive defendant	83 per cent
Unattractive plaintiff and attractive defendant	41 per cent
Unattractive plaintiff and unattractive defendant	69 per cent

IMPLICATIONS The results clearly show that a guilty judgement was most likely when the female secretary was attractive and the male boss was unattractive. A guilty verdict was least likely when the female secretary was unattractive and the male boss was attractive. It appears that the jury inferred that the defendant was less likely to be guilty if the plaintiff was unattractive. This supports the idea that juries make judgements about the motives and character of the defendant based on appearance.

Glossary

actor-observer effect   See fundamental attribution bias.

adversarial system   A trial procedure in which prosecution and defence teams compete to establish the truth of their version of events.

age regression   A hypnotic technique in which the witness is 'taken back' to the age at which they witnessed a crime in order to 'relive it'.

amygdala   A brain structure, part of the limbic system, which is involved in empathic responses to others. The functioning of the amygdala is thought to be impaired in psychopaths.

anger management   An attempt to reduce aggressive behaviour by helping violent offenders to deal with inappropriate feelings of anger.

attributions   The reasons assigned by an individual to explain why something has occurred. Attributions may have little to do with the real reason why something happened.

attribution theory   A branch of psychology that aims to explain how people arrive at attributions.

behavioural evidence   Evidence from the disposition of clues at the crime scene that indicates how the crime was committed.

British Crime Survey (BCS)   A victimisation survey carried out periodically by the Home Office in an attempt to discover the true incidence of crime in the UK.

cognitive-behavioural therapy   A form of psychological therapy that aims to alter maladaptive thinking strategies through behavioural techniques.

cognitive interview   An interview procedure based on the principles of cue-dependent forgetting. It is claimed to enhance recall and produce fewer errors than the standard interview procedure.

commuter   An offender who travels some distance to offend.

conspecifics   Members of the same species.

copycat crime   A crime which is purportedly carried out in the style of another crime, real or fictional.

crime rate   The incidence of crime for a given geographical area, usually expressed as the number of crimes per head of population per year.

crime scene analysis   The offender profiling approach developed in the US by the FBI. Offenders are assigned to categories based on their behaviour at a crime scene.

criminal consistency hypothesis   The view that the behaviour of an offender during the committing of a crime will reflect their behaviour in everyday life.

criminological psychology   The application of psychological research to criminal behaviour.

criminology   The study of criminal behaviour. It encompasses a variety of disciplines including psychology, sociology and law.

dark figure   The proportion of crimes that are committed but which are not detected by official crime statistics.

defensible space   Areas (for example, of a residential development) that appear to belong to someone, having clear boundaries against outsiders and characterised by high levels of natural surveillance.

demand characteristics   The cues that are present in an experimental situation that participants may use in order to work out the experimental aim. There is a danger that participants may alter their behaviour in response to demand characteristics, invalidating the experiment.

deterministic   Describes any theory which suggests that people do not have freedom of choice over their actions.

deviance amplification   The tendency of media sources to 'over-report' certain types of crime (e.g. murder), potentially leading members of the public to have an exaggerated idea of the frequency of such crimes.

dispositional attribution   Attributing someone's behaviour to factors internal to them (e.g. personality).

dizygotic twins   Non-identical twins, sharing the same amount of genetic information as any two siblings.

DNA profiling   The use of DNA evidence from crime scenes to identify offenders, link different crimes and eliminate suspects from an enquiry.

DSM-III-R   *The Diagnostic and Statistical Manual of Psychological Disorders* (third edition, revised). A widely used scheme for classifying and diagnosing psychological disorders, now superseded by *DSM-IV*.

ecological validity   The extent to which an experimental situation resembles the real-life situation to which researchers wish to generalise. Research that is low in ecological validity may not generalise well to real-life situations.

evidential   Relating to evidence as presented in court.

expert evidence   Legal evidence from an acknowledged expert which is given particular weight because of their expertise.

extra-evidential   Relating to factors (e.g. the appearance of the defendant) other than the evidence presented in courts.

forensic hypnosis   The use of hypnotic techniques in an attempt to improve witness reliability.

forensic psychology   The application of psychological research to the legal system.

fundamental attribution bias   The tendency to make situational attributions for our own behaviour and dispositional ones for others' behaviour.

hedonic relevance   A phenomenon whereby our attributions change depending on the degree of relevance a situation has for us.

incidence of crime   The number of crimes that are committed.

inquisitorial system   An alternative trial procedure to the adversarial system, in which the presiding judge(s) controls proceedings, examines witnesses and directs the gathering of evidence.

interrogation   A police interview carried out for the express purpose of extracting a confession from a suspect.

investigative psychology   The application of psychological principles to analyse crimes and apprehend offenders.

juror bias scale   A technique for measuring the degree of prejudice and bias in potential jurors.

just world hypothesis   The belief, held by some people, that the world is a fair and just place in which people deserve the things that happen to them.

labelling theory   The view that the label that is applied to an individual by others (e.g. 'criminal') can influence their behaviour.

locus of control   The extent to which a person feels they are in charge of their own destiny.

marauder   An offender who operates from a home base.

maternal deprivation theory   The view, associated with the work of John Bowlby, that deviant behaviour in adulthood is the result of separation from the attachment figure early in life.

model   In social learning theory (SLT), a person whose behaviour is observed in order to learn it.

monozygotic twins   Identical twins, who share 100 per cent of their genetic information.

offender profiling   The use of crime scene evidence to make educated guesses about the likely characteristics of an offender.

Police and Criminal Evidence Act (PACE)   An Act of Parliament passed in 1984 that, amongst other things, limited the ways in which police interrogations can be carried out.

prevalence of crime   The number of people in the population involved in committing crimes. Variations in the crime rate can be the result of variations in prevalence (e.g. more people committing crimes) or incidence (e.g. the same number of people committing more crimes).

psycho-legal studies   A branch of forensic psychology concerned with legal processes such as jury decision making.

psychological autopsy   The use of crime scene and psychological evidence to work out possible causes of death.

psychometric testing   The measurement of psychological characteristics, usually through the use of questionnaires or inventories. Such tests may concern intelligence (IQ) or personality and generally yield numerical measurements of the attribute being investigated.

psychopath   An individual who appears to lack anxiety and guilt and is typically prone to impulsive and aggressive behaviour. Such individuals are likely to become involved in crime although it should be stressed that not all psychopaths become criminals.

rational choice theory (RCT)   An approach to understanding criminality that emphasises the role of rational processes in the decision to commit a crime.

reconstructive memory   The view that memories, rather than being accurate accounts of events, are 'imaginative reconstructions' based on schematic knowledge.

schema   A cognitive structure into which knowledge is organised in order to make sense of objects, people and situations in the world.

self-fulfilling prophecy   A prediction that comes true because it has been made. Related to labelling theory.

self-serving attribution bias   The tendency to attribute our successes to dispositional factors and our failures to situational ones.

situational attribution   Attributing someone's behaviour to factors external to them.

social cognition   The processes by which we make sense of other people and their actions.

social learning theory   The view that behaviour is primarily learned from observations of models.

social skills training   An attempt to reduce aggressive behaviour by equipping offenders with the skills to manage interactions more effectively.

socio-economic status (SES)   A way of classifying people in terms of their occupational background and economic circumstances. Low SES generally implies manual or semi/unskilled occupation, lower income and fewer years in education, high SES the converse.

somatotype   Bodily build, classified as endomorph (fat), ectomorph (thin) and mesomorph (muscular). According to some early theorists, such as Sheldon, different personality types are associated with the different somatotypes.

Special Weapons and Tactics (SWAT)   In the US, a branch of the police force involved mainly in special operations, such as hostage-taking incidents.

standard interview procedure   The usual method by which police interviews are conducted.

story order   An evidence strategy in which witnesses appear in the sequence in which events occurred. Considered more effective than witness order.

television technique   A hypnotic technique in which a witness is encouraged to imagine an event as if seen on television.

testosterone   A male sex hormone the main role of which is to promote sexual development and behaviour. However, it may also influence a range of other behaviours including aggression.

token economy   An attempt to reduce offending behaviour by selectively reinforcing desirable behaviours within an institution.

VICAP   The Violent Criminal Apprehension Programme. An FBI database of violent offences used to generate offender profiles.

victim derogation   The tendency to blame a victim for their own misfortune. Related to belief in a just world (see just world hypothesis).

victimisation survey   A technique for measuring the crime rate which, instead of relying on crime statistics as reported by the police, surveys a sample of the population about their experiences of crime. Victimisation surveys typically reveal a higher incidence of crime than police figures.

violence distraction   The tendency for witnesses of violent events to provide poorer testimony than witnesses of non-violent events, either because of the detrimental effect of arousal on memory or possibly due to weapon focus.

weapon focus   The tendency for witnesses of violent crimes to focus on the weapon used, generally resulting in poorer recall of other aspects of the event.

witness order   An evidence strategy in which witnesses appear in the order deemed most likely to persuade the jury. Considered less effective than story order.

zero tolerance   An approach to the prevention of serious crime based on vigorous police response to minor infractions of the law.

References

Adlam, R.C.A. (1981) 'The police personality' in D.W. Pope and N.L.Weiner (eds) *Modern Policing*. London: Croom Helm.

Ageton, S. and Elliot, D. (1974) 'The effects of legal processing on self-concept' *Social Problems*, 22, 87–100.

Aggleton, J.P. and Waskett, L. (1999) 'The ability of odours to serve as state-dependent cues for real-world memories. Can Viking smells aid the recall of Viking experiences?' *British Journal of Psychology*, 90, 1–8.

Aiken T. W., Stumphauzer, J.S. and Veloz, E.V. (1977) 'Behavioral analysis of non-delinquent brothers in a high juvenile crime community' *Behavioral Disorders*, 2, 221–222.

Ainsworth, P.B. (1998) *Psychology, Law and Eyewitness Testimony*. Chichester: Wiley.

—— (2000) *Psychology and Crime: Myths and Reality*. Harlow: Pearson Education.

—— (2001) *Offender Profiling and Crime Analysis*. Cullumpton: Willan.

Alper, A., Buckhout, R., Chern, S., Harwood, R. and Slomivits, M. (1976) 'Eyewitness identification: accuracy of individual vs. composite recollection of a crime' *Bulletin of the Psychonomic Society*, 8, 147–149.

Arbuthnot, J., Gordon, D.A. and Jurkovic, G.J. (1987) 'Personality' in H.C.Quay (ed.) *Handbook of Juvenile Delinquency*. Chichester: Wiley.

Aronson, E., Wilson, T.D. and Akert, R.M. (1997) *Social Psychology* (second edition). New York: Addison-Wesley.

Atkinson, M. (1984) *Our Masters' Voices: The Language and Body Language of Politics*. London: Routledge.

Austin, T.L., Hale, D.C. and Ramsey, L.J. (1987) 'The effect of layoff on police authoritarianism' *Criminal Justice and Behaviour*, 14, 194–210.

Ayllon, T. and Milan, M.A. (1979) *Correctional rehabilitation and management: a psychological approach*. New York: Wiley.

Bandura, A. (1986) *Social foundations of thought and action*. Englewood Cliffs, NJ: Prentice-Hall.

Bandura, A., Ross, D. and Ross, S.A. (1963) 'Imitation of film-mediated aggressive models' *Journal of Abnormal and Social Psychology*, 1, 589–595.

Baron, A.B. and Byrne, D. (1994) *Social Psychology: Understanding Human Interaction* (seventh edition). Boston: Allyn & Bacon.

Bartlett, F. C. (1932) *Remembering*. Cambridge: Cambridge University Press.

Bayley, D.H. (1979) 'Police functions, structure and control in Western Europe and North America: comparative and historical studies' in N. Morris and M. Tonry (eds) *Crime and Justice: An annual review of research,* Vol.1. Chicago: University of Chicago Press.

Belson, W.A. (1975) *Juvenile theft: the causal factors*. New York: Harper Collins and Row.

—— (1978) *Television violence and the adolescent boy*. Farnborough: Saxon House.

Bennett, T. and Wright, R. (1984) *Burglars on burglary: prevention and the offender*. Aldershot: Gower.

Berkowitz, L. (1969) 'The frustration-aggression hypothesis revisited' in L. Berkowitz (ed.) *Roots of Aggression: a re-examination of the frustration-aggression hypothesis*. New York: Atherton Press.

Black, D.J. and Reiss, A. (1970) 'Police control of juveniles' *American Sociological Review*, 35, 63–77.

Blackburn, R. (1993) *The Psychology of Criminal Conduct*. Chichester: John Wiley and Sons.

—— (1996) 'What is Forensic Psychology?' *Legal and Criminological Psychology*, 1, 3–16.

Blair, R.J.R., Morris, J.S., Firth, C.D., Perrett, D.I. and Dolan, R.J. (1999) 'Dissociable neural responses to facial expressions of sadness and anger' *Brain*, 122, 883–893.

Bohman, M., Cloninger, C.R., Sigvarsson, S. and von Knorring, A. (1982) 'Predisposition to petty criminality in Swedish adoptees: I. Genetic and environmental heterogeneity' *Archives of General Psychiatry*, 39, 1233 – 1241.

Boon, J. and Davies, G.M. (1992) 'Fact and fiction in offender profiling' *Issues in Legal and Criminological Psychology*, 32, 3–9.

Bottomley, K. and Pease, K. (1986) *Crime and punishment: interpreting the data*. Milton Keynes: Open University Press.

Bowlby, J. (1951) *Maternal Care and Mental Health: Report to World Health Organisation*. New York: Shoken Books.

Box, S. (1983) *Power, crime and mystification*. London: Tavistock.

Brantingham, P.J. and Faust, F.L. (1976) 'A conceptual model of crime prevention' *Crime and Delinquency*, 22, 130–146.

Bratton, W.J. (1998) 'Crime is down in New York City: Blame the police' in N. Dennis (ed.) *Zero Tolerance: Policing in a Free Society*. London: IEA Health and Welfare Unit.

Brewer, K. (2000) *Psychology and Crime*. Oxford: Heinemann.

Brigham, J.C. & Pfeiffer, J.E. (1994) 'Evaluating the fairness of line ups' in D.F. Ross, J.D. Read and M.P. Toglia (eds) *Adult Eyewitness Testimony: Trends and Developments*. Cambridge: Cambridge University Press.

Brown, J. M. (1997) 'Psychology at the Service of the Police' *Proceedings of the 15th ATP Conference*, July 1997, pp. 21–27.

Bruce, V. (1988) *Recognising Faces*. Hove: Lawrence Earlbaum Associates.

Brussel, J.A. (1968) *Casebook of a Crime Psychiatrist*. London: New English Library.

Buckhout, R., Figueroa, D. and Koff, E. (1975) 'Eyewitness identification: effects of suggestion and bias in identification from photographs' *Bulletin of the Psychonomic Society*, 6, 71–74.

Burrows, J. (1980) 'Closed circuit television and crime on the London Underground' in R.V.G. Clarke and P. Mayhew (eds) *Designing Out Crime*. London: HMSO.

Caddo-Bossier Sheriff's Office (1997) *Guidelines for Media Coverage of Hostage Negotiations*. Press release to local media.
http://www.caddosheriff.org/pr/releases/backgrnd/negot.htm

Caldwell, R.G. (1965) *Criminology* (second edition). New York: Ronald Press.

Calhoun, F.S. and Brooks, S.W. (1997) *To the barricades: hostages, standoffs and the failure of history*. Unpublished manuscript, cited in Hogan (1998).

Canter, D. (1989) 'Offender profiles' *The Psychologist*, 2, 12–16.

—— (2000) 'Offender profiling and criminal differentiation' *Legal and Criminological Psychology*, 5, 23–46.

Canter, D. and Gregory, A. (1994) 'Identifying the residential location of rapists' *Journal of the Forensic Science Society*, 34, 169–175.

Canter, D. and Heritage, R. (1990) 'A multivariate model of sexual offence behaviour: developments in "offender profiling"' *Journal of Forensic Psychiatry*, 1, 185–212.

Castellow, W.A., Wuensch, K.L. and Moore, C.H (1990) 'Effects of physical attractiveness of the plaintiff and defendant in sexual harassment judgements' *Journal of Social Behaviour and Personality*, 5, 547–562.

Christiansen, K.O. (1977) 'A preliminary study of criminality among twins' in S.A. Mednick and K.O. Christiansen (eds) *Biosocial Bases of Criminal Behaviour*. New York: Gardiner Press.

Clifford, B.R. and Hollin, C.R. (1981) 'Effects of the type of incident and the number of perpetrators on eyewitness memory' *Journal of Applied Psychology*, 66, 364–370.

Clifford, B.R. and Richards, V.J. (1977) 'Comparison of recall of police and civilians under conditions of long and short durations of exposure' *Perceptual and Motor Skills*, 45, 503–512.

Clifford, B.R. and Scott, J. (1978) 'Individual and situational factors in eyewitness memory' *Journal of Applied Psychology*, 63, 352–359.

Cloninger, C.R., Christiansen, K.O., Reich, T. and Gottesman, I.I. (1978) 'Implications of sex differences in the prevalence of antisocial personality, alcoholism and criminality for familial transmission' *Archives of General Psychiatry*, 35, 941–951.

Cohen, H.L. and Filipcjak, J. (1971) *A new learning environment*. San Francisco: Jossey Bass.

Committee on Ethical Guidelines for Forensic Psychologists (1991) 'Speciality guidelines for forensic psychologists' *Law and Human Behaviour*, 15, 261–268.

Copson, G. (1995) *Coals to Newcastle? Police Research Group Special Interest Papers: Paper 7*. London: Home Office.

Cornish, D.B. and Clark, R.V. (1987) 'Understanding crime displacement: the application of rational choice theory' *Criminology*, 25, 933–947.

Cortes, J.B. and Gatti, F.M. (1972) *Delinquency and Crime: A Biopsychosocial Approach*. New York: Seminar Press.

Crowe, R.R. (1972) 'The adopted offspring of women criminal offenders' *Archives of General Psychiatry*, 27, 600–603.

Cruse, D. and Leigh, B.S. (1987) '"Adam's Rib" revisited: legal and non-legal influences on the processing of trial information' *Social Behaviour*, 2, 221–230.

Cumberbatch, G. (1989) 'Violence and the mass media: the research evidence' in G. Cumberbatch and D. Howitt *A measure of uncertainty: the effects of the mass media*. London: Broadcasting Standards Council/John Libbey.

Cutler, B.L. and Penrod, S. (1995) *Mistaken Identification: The Eyewitness, Psychology and the Law*. New York: Cambridge University Press.

Dalgaard, O.S. and Kringlen, E. (1976) 'A Norwegian twin study of criminality' *British Journal of Criminology*, 16, 213–233.

Dane, F.C. and Wrightsman, L.S. (1982) 'Effects of defendants' and victims' characteristics on jurors' verdicts' in N.L. Kerr and R.M. Bray (eds) *The Psychology of the Courtroom*. London: Academic Press.

Davies, G.M. (1991) 'Research on children's testimony: implications for interviewing practice' in C.R. Hollin and K. Howells (eds) *Clinical Applications to Sex Offenders and Their Victims*. Chichester: Wiley.

—— (1999) 'Contamination of witness memory' in A. Heaton-Armstrong, E. Shepherd and E. Wolchover (eds) *Analysing Witness Testimony*. London: Blackstone.

Davies, G.M., Ellis, H.D., and Shepherd, J.W. (1978) 'Face identification: the influence of delay upon accuracy of photofit construction' *Journal of Police Science and Administration*, 6, 35–42.

Davis, R.C. and Friedman, L.N. (1985) 'The emotional aftermath of crime and violence' in C.R. Fingley (ed.) *Trauma and its wake: the study and treatment of post-traumatic stress disorder*. New York: Bruner/Mazel.

Donohoe, W.A. and Roberto, A.J. (1993) 'Relational development as negotiated in hostage negotiation' *Human Communication Research*, 20, 175–198.

Dooley, E. (1990) 'Prison suicide in England and Wales 1972 – 1987' *British Journal of Psychiatry*, 156, 40–45.

Eckman, P. (1985) *Telling lies*. New York: Norton.

Ellis, H.D. (1984) 'Practical aspects of face memory' in G.L. Wells and E.F. Loftus (eds) *Eyewitness Testimony: Psychological Perspectives*. Cambridge: Cambridge University Press.

Ellis, H.D., Shepherd, J. and Davis, G.M. (1975) 'An investigation of the use of photo-fit technique for recalling faces' *British Journal of Psychology*, 66, 25–28.

Epps, P. and Parnell, R.W. (1952) 'Physique and temperament of women delinquents compared to women undergraduates' *British Journal of Medical Psychology*, 25, 249–255.

Evans, R.C. and Koederitz, G.D. (1983) 'The requirement of restitution for juvenile offenders: an alternative disposition' *Journal of Offender Counselling, Services and Rehabilitation*, 7, 1–20.

Eysenck, H.J. (1964) *Crime and Personality*. London: Routledge & Kegan Paul.

Eysenck, M.W. (1993) *Principles of Cognitive Psychology*. Hove: Lawrence Earlbaum Associates.

—— (1996) *Simply Psychology*. Hove: Taylor & Francis.

Eysenck, M.W. and Keane, M.T. (1995) *Cognitive Psychology: A Student's Handbook* (third edition). Hove: Psychology Press.

Farrington, D.P., Biron, L. and LeBlanc, M. (1982) 'Personality and delinquency in London and Montreal' in J. Gunn and D.P. Farrington (eds) *Abnormal Offenders, Delinquency and the Criminal Justice System*. Chichester: Wiley.

Farrington, D.P. and Nutall, C.P. (1980) 'Prison size, overcrowding, violence and recidivism' *Journal of Criminal Justice*, 8, 221–231.

Feindler, E.L., Marriott, S.A. and Iweta, M. (1984) 'Group anger control training for junior high school delinquents' *Cognitive Therapy and Research*, 8, 299–311.

Feldman, M.P. (1977) *Criminal behaviour: a psychological analysis*. Chichester: Wiley.

Feldman, P. (1993) *The Psychology of Crime*. Cambridge: Cambridge University Press.

Feldmann, T.B. (2001) *Hostage Negotiation Research*. University of Louisville Department of Psychiatry and Medicine
http://members.aol.com/_ht_a/tbfeld/index.html

Fenster, C.A., Wiedeman, C.F. and Locke, B. (1973) 'Police personality, social science folklore and psychological measurement' in B. Sales (ed.) *Psychology in the Legal Process*. New York: Spectrum.

Fisher, R.P., Geiselman, R.E. and Amador, M. (1990) 'A field test of the cognitive interview: enhancing the recollection of actual victims and witnesses of crime' *Journal of Applied Psychology*, 74, 722–727.

Fisher, R.P., Geiselman, R.E., Raymond, D.S., Jurkevich, L.M. and Warhaftif, M.L. (1987) 'Enhancing enhanced eyewitness memory: refining the cognitive interview' *Journal of Police Science and Administration*, 15, 291–297.

Garland, D. (1997) 'Of crime and criminals: the development of Criminology in Britain' in M. Maguire, R. Morgan and R. Reiner (eds) *The Oxford Handbook of Criminology* (second edition). Oxford: Oxford University Press.

Geiselman, R.E., Fisher, R.P., MacKinnon, D.F. and Holland, H.L. (1985) 'Eyewitness memory enhancement in police interview: cognitive retrieval mnemonics versus hypnosis' *Journal of Applied Psychology*, 70, 401–412.

Geiselman, R.E., Fisher, R.P., MacKinnon, D.F. and Holland, H.L. (1986) 'Enhancement of eyewitness memory with the cognitive interview' *American Journal of Psychology*, 99, 385–401.

Geiselman, R.E., Saywitz, K.J. and Bernstein, G.K. (1990) *Cognitive Interviewing Techniques for Child Victims and Witnesses of Crime*. Report to the State Justice Institute, Torrence, California.

Gibbens, D.C. and Krohn, M.D. (1986) *Delinquent Behaviour* (fourth edition). Englewood Cliffs, NJ: Prentice-Hall.

Gibbens, T.C.N. (1963) *Psychiatric Studies of Borstal Lads*. Maudsley Monographs No. 11. London: Oxford University Press.

Gibbs, L.E. (1974) 'Effects of juvenile legal procedures on juvenile offenders' self-attitudes' *Journal of Research in Crime and Delinquency*, 11, 51–55.

Gibson, H.B. (1982) 'The use of hypnosis in police investigations' *Bulletin of the British Psychological Society*, 35, 138–142.

Glaser, D. (1983) 'Supervising offenders outside of prison' in J.Q. Wilson (ed.) *Crime and Public Policy*. San Francisco: ICS Press.

Goldstein, A.P. (1986) 'Psychological skill training and the aggressive adolescent' in S.J. Apter and A.P. Goldstein (eds) *Youth Violence: Programmes and Prospects*. New York: Plenum.

Goldstein, A.P., Glick, B., Irwin, M.J., Pask-McCartney, C. and Rubama, I. (1989) *Reducing delinquency: intervention in the community*. New York: Pergamon.

Gorden, R. (1975) *Interviewing: Strategy, Techniques and Tactics*. Homewood, Il: Dorsey.

Gordon, R.A. (1990) 'Attributions for blue-collar and white-collar crime: the effects of subject and defendant race on simulated juror decisions' *Journal of Applied Social Psychology*, 20, 971–983.

Gordon, R.A., Bindrim, T., McNicholas, M. and Walden, T. (1988) 'Perceptions of blue-collar and white-collar crime: the effect of defendant race on simulated juror decisions' *Journal of Social Psychology*, 128, 191–197.

Grabowski, P.N. (1999) *Zero Tolerance Policing*. Trends and Issues in Criminal Justice Paper No. 102. Canberra: Australian Institute of Criminology.

Gross, R.D. (1991) *Psychology: the Science of Mind and Behaviour* (second edition). London: Hodder & Stoughton.

—— (1996) *Psychology: The Science of Mind and Behaviour* (third edition). London: Hodder & Stoughton.

Groth, A.N., Burgess, A.W. and Holmstrom, L.L. (1977) 'Rape, power, anger and sexuality' *American Journal of Psychiatry*, 134, 1239–1248.

Gudjonsson, G.H. (1990) 'Self-deception and other-deception in forensic assessment' *Personality and Individual Differences*, 11, 219–225.

—— (1992) *The Psychology of Interrogations, Confessions and Testimony*. Chichester: Wiley.

Gudjonsson, G.H. and Adlam, K.R.C. (1983) 'Personality patterns of British police officers' *Personality and Individual Differences*, 4, 507–512.

Hammer, M., Van Zandt, C.R. and Rogan, R.G. (1994) 'Crisis/hostage negotiation team profile' *FBI Law Enforcement Bulletin*, 63 (3), 8–15.

Hans, V.P. and Vladmir, N. (1986) *Judging the Jury*. New York: Plenum.

Harrower, J. (1996) 'Criminal Psychology' in H. Coolican (ed.) *Applied Psychology*. London: Hodder & Stoughton.

—— (1998) *Applying Psychology to Crime*. London: Hodder & Stoughton.

Hartl, E.M., Monnelly, E.P. and Elderkin, R. (1982) *Physique and delinquent behaviour: a thirty-year follow-up of William H. Sheldon's varieties of delinquent youth.* New York: Academic Press.

Hastie, R., Penrod, S.D. and Pennington, N. (1983) *Inside The Jury.* Cambridge, Mass: Harvard University Press.

Haward, L.R.C. (1981) *Forensic Psychology.* London: Batsford.

Hazelwood, R.R. (1987) 'Analyzing the rape and profiling the offender' in R.R. Hazelwood and A.W. Burgess (eds) *Practical Aspects of Rape Investigation: A Multidisciplinary Approach.* New York: Elsevier.

Heather, N. (1977) 'Personal illness in lifers and the effects of long-term indeterminate sentences' *British Journal of Criminology*, 17, 378–386.

Hewstone, M., Stroebe, W. and Stephenson, G.M. (1996) *Introduction to Social Psychology* (second edition). Oxford: Blackwell.

Hindelang, M.J., Hirschi, T. and Weis, J.G. (1981) *Measuring Delinquency.* Beverly Hills, CA: Sage.

Hobbs, T.R. and Holt, M.N. (1976) 'The effects of token reinforcement on the behaviour of delinquents in cottage settings' *Journal of Applied Behaviour Analysis*, 9, 189–198.

Hollin, C. R. (1989) *Psychology and Crime: An Introduction to Criminological Psychology.* London: Routledge.

—— (1995) 'Forensic (criminological) psychology' in A.M. Colman (ed.) *Applications of Psychology.* London: Longman.

Hollin, C.R. and Clifford, B.R. (1983) 'Eyewitness testimony: the effects of discussion on recall accuracy and agreement' *Journal of Applied Social Psychology*, 13, 234–244.

Holmes, R.M. (1989) *Profiling Violent Crimes: An Investigative Tool.* Newbury Park: Sage.

Home Office (1994) *Criminal Statistics.* London: Home Office.

Horne, C.J. (1996) 'The case for: CCTV should be introduced' *International Journal of Risk, Security and Crime Prevention*, 1, 317–326.

Hough, M. and Mayhew, P. (1983) *The British Crime Survey: First Report.* Home Office Research Study Number 76. London: HMSO.

Hovland, C.L. and Janis, I.L. (1959) *Communication and Persuasion: Psychological Studies of Opinion Change.* New Haven, CT: Yale University Press.

Howitt, D. (1998) *Crime, the media and the law*. Chichester: Wiley.

Huizinga, D. and Elliot, D.S. (1987) *Self-reported measures of delinquency and crime: methodological issues and comparative findings*. Boulder, CO: Behavioural Research Institute.

Hutchings, B. and Mednick, S.A. (1975) 'Registered criminality in the adoptive and biological parents of registered male criminal adoptees' in R.R. Fieve, D. Rosenthal and H. Brill (eds), *Genetic Research in Psychiatry*. Baltimore: Johns Hopkins University Press.

Inbau, F.E., Reid, J.A. and Buckley, J.P. (1986) *Criminal interrogation and confessions* (third edition). Baltimore: Williams and Wilkins.

Irving, B.L. and McKenzie, I.K. (1989) *Police interrogation: the effects of the Police and Criminal Evidence Act*. London: Police Foundation.

Jackson, J.L., van den Eshof, P. and DeHeuver, E.E. (1997) 'A research approach to offender profiling' in J.L. Jackson and D.A. Bekerian (eds), *Offender Profiling: Theory, Research and Practice*. Chichester: Wiley.

Jahoda, G. (1954) 'A note on Ashanti names and their relation to personality' *British Journal of Psychology*, 45, 192–195.

Jenkins, J.G. and Dallenbach, K.M. (1924) 'Oblivience during sleeping and waking' *American Journal of Psychology*, 35, 605–612.

Jones, D.P.H. (1987) 'The evidence of a three year old child' *Criminal Law Review*, 677–681.

—— (1988) *Interviewing the Sexually Abused Child*. London: Gaskell.

Jones, D.P.H. and McGraw, J.M. (1987) 'Reliable and fictitious accounts of sexual abuse to children' *Journal of Interpersonal Violence*, 2, 27–45.

Kahn, A. (1984) *Victims of violence: final report of APA taskforce on the victims of crime and violence*. Washington: American Psychological Association.

Kalat, J.W. (1998) *Biological Psychology* (sixth edition). Pacific Grove, CA: Brooks Cole.

Kassin, S.M. and Wrightsman, L.S. (1983) 'The construction and validation of a juror bias scale' *Journal of Research in Personality*, 17, 423–442.

Kelling, G.L. and Coles, C.M. (1996) *Fixing broken windows: restoring order and reducing crime in our communities*. New York: Free Press.

Klein, M.W. (1986) 'Labelling theory and delinquency policy: an experimental test' *Criminal Justice and Behaviour*, 13, 47–79.

Klinke, C.L. and Meyer, C. (1990) 'Evaluation of rape victim by men and women with high and low belief in a just world' *Psychology of Women Quarterly*, 14, 343–353.

Kohlberg, L. (1976) 'Moral stages and moralisation: The cognitive-developmental approach' in T.Lickona (ed.) *Moral Development and Behaviour*. New York: Holt, Reinhart & Winston.

Kuehn, L. (1974) 'Looking down a gun barrel: person perception and violent crime' *Perceptual and Motor Skills*, 39(1), 159–164.

Landau, S.F. (1981) 'Juveniles and the police' *British Journal of Criminology*, 21, 27–46.

Laughery, K.R. and Fowler, R.H. (1980) 'Sketch artist and Identikit procedures for recalling faces' *Journal of Applied Psychology*, 65, 307–316.

Leippe, M.R., Manion, A.P. and Roamanczyk, A. (1992) 'Persuasion: how and how well do fact finders judge the accuracy of adults and children's memory' *Journal of Personality and Social Psychology*, 63, 181–197.

Lerner, M.J. (1970) 'The desire for justice and reactions to victims' in J.McCauley and L.Berkowitz (eds) *Altruism and Helping Behaviour*. Orlando, FL: Academic Press.

—— (1980) *The Belief in a Just World: a fundamental decision*. New York: Plenum.

Lerner, M.J. and Miller, D.T. (1978) 'Just world research and the attribution process: looking back and ahead' *Psychological Bulletin*, 85, 1030–1051.

Lipsey, J.W. (1992) 'Juvenile delinquency treatment: a meta-analytical enquiry into the variability of effects' in T. Cook (ed.) *Meta-Analysis for Explanation: A Casebook*. New York: Russel Sage Foundation.

Loftus, E. F. and Palmer, J.C. (1974) 'Reconstruction of automobile destruction: an example of the interaction between language and memory' *Journal of Verbal Learning and Verbal Behaviour*, 13, 585–589.

Loftus, E. F., Loftus, G.R. and Messo, J. (1987) 'Some facts about "weapon focus"' *Law and Human Behaviour*, 11, 55–62.

Loftus, E.F. and Zanni, G.R. (1975) 'Eyewitness testimony: the influence of the wording of the question' *Bulletin of the Psychonomic Society*, 5(1), 86–88.

Loftus, E.F., Greene, E.L. and Doyle, J.M. (1990) 'The psychology of eyewitness testimony' in D.C. Raskin (ed.) *Psychological Methods in Criminal Investigations and Evidence*. New York: Springer.

Logan, M. (1998) *What facilitates or hinders successful crisis negotiation?* Royal Canadian Mounted Police
http://www.rcmp-learning.org/docs/ecdd1216.htm

Lombroso, C. (1876) *L'uomo Delinquente*. Turin: Fraticelli Bocca.

Lundman, R.J., Sykes, R.E. and Clark, J.P. (1978) 'Police control of juveniles: a replication' *Journal of Research in Crime and Delinquency*, 15, 74–91.

Maass, A. and Kohnen, A. (1989) 'Eyewitness identification: simulating the "weapon effect"' *Law and Human Behaviour*, 13, 397–409.

McDowell, C.P. (1987) 'Suicide disguised as murder: a dimension of Munchausen Syndrome' *Journal of Forensic Psychology*, 32, 254–261.

Maguire, M. (1997) 'Crime statistics, patterns and trends: changing perspectives and their implications' in M. Maguire, R. Morgan and R. Reiner (eds) *The Oxford Handbook of Criminology* (second edition). Oxford: Oxford University Press.

Males, M. and Macallair, D. (1998) 'The effect of juvenile curfew laws in California' *Western Criminology Review*, 1, 1.

Marshall, R.J. (1983) 'A psychoanalytic perspective on the diagnosis and development of juvenile delinquency' in W.S. Laufer and J.M. Day (eds) *Personality Theory, Moral Development and Criminal Behaviour*. Lexington: Heath.

Matthews, V.M. (1968) 'Differential Association: an empirical note' *Social Problems*, 14, 376–383.

Meichenbaum, D.H., Bowers, K.S. and Ross, R.R. (1969) 'A behavioural analysis of the teacher expectancy effect' *Journal of Personality and Social Psychology*, 13, 306–316.

Milarsky, J.R., Kessler, R.C., Stipp, H. and Rubens, W.S. (1982) *Television and aggression: a panel study*. New York: Academic Press.

Mirabella, R.W. and Trudeau, J. (1981) 'Managing hostage negotiations' *The Police Chief*, 48 (5), 45–48.

Mirrlees-Black, C., Budd, T., Partridge, S. and Mayhew, P. (1998) *The 1998 British Crime Survey, England and Wales*. Home Office Statistical Bulletin 21/98. London: Home Office.

Mischel, W. (1968) *Personality and Assessment*. New York: Wiley.

Mitchell, D. and Blair, R.J.R. (1999) 'State of the art: psychopathy' *The Psychologist* 13(7), 356–360.

Moon, J.R. and Eisler, R.M. (1983) 'Anger control: an experimental comparison of three behavioural treatments' *Behaviour Therapy*, 14, 493–505.

Moran, G. and Cutler, B.L. (1991) 'The prejudicial impact of pre-trial publicity' *Journal of Applied Social Psychology*, 21, 345–367.

Moston, S. (1990a) *The ever-so-gentle art of police interrogation*. Paper presented at the British Psychological Society annual conference, Swansea University, 5 April.

—— (1990b) 'How children interpret and respond to questions and situation sources of suggestibility in eyewitness interviews' *Social Behaviour*, 5, 155–167.

Munsterberg, H. (1908) *On the Witness Stand: Essays on Psychology and Crime*. New York: Clark, Boardman.

Newman, O. (1973) *Defensible space: crime prevention through urban design*. New York: Macmillan.

Nietzel, M.T. (1979) *Crime and its modification: a social learning perspective*. New York: Pergamon.

Novaco, R.W. (1975) *Anger control: the development and evaluation of an experimental treatment*. Lexington: D.C. Health.

Oldfield, M. (1996) *The Kent Reconviction Survey*. Maidstone: Kent Probation Service.

Osborn, S.G. and West, D.J. (1979) 'Conviction records of fathers and sons compared' *British Journal of Criminology*, 19, 120–133.

Padawer-Singer, A.M. and Barton, A. (1974) 'The Impact of Pre-trial Publicity on Jurors Verdicts' in R.J. Simon (ed.) *The Jury System in America: A Critical Overview*. Beverly Hills, CA: Sage.

Pearse, J. and Gudjonsson, G.H. (1999) 'Measuring influential police interviewing tactics: a factor analytic approach' *Legal and Criminological Psychology*, 4, 221–238.

Pennington, N. and Hastie, R. (1988) 'Explanation-based decision making: effects of memory structure on judgement' *Journal of Experimental Psychology: Learning, Memory and Cognition*, 14, 521–533.

—— (1990) 'Practical implications of psychological research on juror and jury decision making' *Personality and Social Psychology Bulletin*, 16, 90–105.

—— (1993) 'Reasoning in explanation-based decision making' *Cognition*, 49, 123–163.

Penrod, S.D. and Cutler, B.L. (1987) 'Assessing the Competence of Juries' in I.B. Weiner and A.K. Hess (eds) *Handbook of Forensic Psychology*. New York: Wiley.

Penry, J. (1971) *Looking at Faces and Remembering Them*. London: Elek Books.

Pfeiffer, J.E. and Ogloff, J.R. (1991) 'Ambiguity and guilt determinations: a modern racist perspective' *Journal of Applied Social Psychology*, 21, 1713–1725.

Piaget, J. (1959) *Language and the thought of the child*. London: Routledge & Kegan Paul.

Piliavin, I. and Briar, S. (1964) 'Police encounters with juveniles' *American Journal of Sociology*, 70, 206–214.

Povey, D. and Prime, J. (1998) *Notifiable offences England and Wales April 1997 to March 1998*. Home Office Statistical Bulletin 22/98. London: Home Office.

Putnam W.H. (1979) 'Hypnosis and distortions in eye witness memory' *International Journal of Experimental and Clinical Hypnosis*, 27, 437–448.

Putwain. D.W. and Sammons, A. (2001) *A2 Level Psychology in a Week*. London: Letts Educational.

Rasch, W. (1981) 'The effects of indeterminate detention: a study of men sentenced to life imprisonment' *International Journal of Law and Psychiatry*, 4, 417–431.

Reiser, M. (1990) 'Investigative Hypnosis' in D.C. Raskin (ed.) *Psychological Methods in Criminal Investigations and Evidence*. New York: Springer.

Ressler, R.K., Burgess, A.W. and Douglas, J. (1988) *Sexual Homicide: Patterns and Motives*. Lexington: Lexington Books.

Rettig, S. (1966) 'Ethical risk taking in group and individual conditions' *Journal of Personality and Social Psychology*, 4, 648–654.

Roshier, R. (1995) *A comparative study of reconviction rates in Cleveland*. Middlesborough: Cleveland Probation Service.

Rotter, J.B. (1966) 'Generalised expectancies for internal versus external control of reinforcement' *Psychological Monographs*, 80, (1, whole no. 609).

Rushton, J.F. and Christjohn, R.D. (1981) 'Extraversion, neuroticism, psychoticism and self-reported delinquency: evidence from eight separate samples' *Personality and Individual Differences*, 2, 11–20.

Rutter, M. (1971) *Maternal deprivation reassessed*. Harmondsworth: Penguin.

Rutter, M. and Giller, H. (1983) *Juvenile delinquency: trends and perspectives*. Harmondsworth: Penguin.

Saks, M. (1977) *Jury Verdicts*. Lexington, Mass: Heath.

Sales, B.D. and Hafemeister, T.L. (1985) 'Law and Psychology' in E.M. Altmaier and M.E. Meyer (eds) *Applied Specialities in Psychology*. London: Lawrence Erlbaum.

Salfati, G. G. (1999) Talk presented at Student Educational Conferences, Westminster, November 1999.

Sarason, I.G. (1978) 'A cognitive social learning approach to juvenile delinquency' in R.D. Hare and D. Schalling (eds) *Psychopathic behaviour: approaches to research*. Chichester: Wiley.

Schafer, S. (1976) *An Introduction to Criminology*. New York: McGraw-Hill.

Schneider, A.L. (1986) 'Restitution and recidivism rates of juvenile offenders: results from four experimental studies' *Criminology*, 24, 533–552.

Scully, D. and Marolla, J. (1984) 'Convicted rapists' vocabulary of motive: excuses and justifications' *Social Problems*, 31, 530–544.

Sellin, T. (1938) *Culture conflict and crime*. New York: Social Science Research Council.

Sergent, J. (1984) An investigation into component and configurational processes underlying face perception. *British Journal of Psychology*, 75, 221–242.

Sheldon, W.H. (1949) *Varieties of Delinquent Youth*. New York: Harper.

Sherman, L. (1997) 'Policing for crime prevention' in L. Sherman, D. Gottfredson, D. MacKenzie, J. Eck, P. Reuter and S. Bushway (eds) *Preventing crime: what works, what doesn't, what's promising*. Report to the United States Congress prepared for the National Institute of Justice http://www.preventingcrime.org/

Smith, D.A. and Visher, C.A. (1982) 'Street level justice: situational determinants of police arrest decisions' *Social Problems*, 29, 167–177.

Softley, P. (1980) *Police interrogation. An observational study in four police stations*. Home Office Research Study No. 61. London: HMSO.

Spence, S.H. and Marzillier, J.S. (1981) 'Social skills training with adolescent male offenders: II Short term, long term and generalisation effects' *Behaviour Research and Therapy*, 19, 349–368.

Steffenmeister, D.J., Allan, E.A., Harer, M.D. and Streifel, C. (1989) 'Age and the distribution of crime' *American Journal of Sociology*, 94, 803–831.

Stephenson, G.M. (1992) *The Psychology of Criminal Justice*. Oxford: Blackwell.

Stott, D. (1982) *Delinquency: the problem and its prevention*. London: Batsford.

Sutherland, E.H. (1939) *Principles of Criminology*. Philadelphia: Lippincott.

—— (1951) 'Critique of Sheldon's varieties of delinquent youth' *American Sociological Review*, 16, 10–13.

Taylor, R.B., Gottfredsen, S.D. and Brower, S. (1980) 'The defensibility of defensible space: a critical review' in T. Hirschi and M. Gottfredsen (eds) *Understanding Crime: Current Theory and Research*. Beverly Hills, CA: Sage.

Thibaut, J. and Walker, L. (1978) 'A Theory of Procedure' *California Law Review*, 66, 541–566.

Thomson, D.M. (1995) 'Eyewitness testimony and identification tests' in N. Brewer and C. Wilson (eds) *Psychology and Policing*. Hillsdale, NJ: L.E.A.

Thornton, D. (1987) 'Moral development theory' in B.J. McGurk and D.M. Thornton (eds) A*pplying psychology to imprisonment: theory and practice*. London: HMSO.

Thornton, D. and Reid, R.L. (1982) 'Moral reasoning and types of criminal offence' *British Journal of Social Psychology*, 21, 231–238.

Tully, B. and Tam, K.O. (1987) 'Helping the police with their enquiries: the development of special care questioning techniques' *Children and Society*, 3, 87–197.

Visher, C.A. (1987) 'Juror decision-making: the importance of evidence' *Law and Human Behaviour*, 11, 1–17.

Wagstaff, G.F. (1983) *Hypnosis, Compliance and Belief*. Brighton: Harvester Press.

Walker, N. and Farrington, D.P. (1981) 'Reconviction rates of adult males after different sentences' *British Journal of Criminology*, 21, 357–360.

Walster, E. (1966) 'The assignment of responsibility for an accident' *Journal of Personality and Social Psychology*, 5, 508–516.

Wells, G.L. and Murray, D.M. (1984) 'Eyewitness Confidence' in G.L. Wells and E.F. Loftus (eds) *Eyewitness Testimony: Psychological Perspectives*. Cambridge: Cambridge University Press.

Werner, J.S., Minkin, N., Minkin, B.L., Fixsen, D.L., Phillips, E.L. and Wolf, M.M. (1975) 'Intervention Package': an analysis to prepare juvenile delinquents for encounters with police officers' *Criminal Justice and Behaviour*, 2, 55–83.

West, D.J. (1982) *Delinquency: its roots, careers and prospects*. Cambridge, Mass: Harvard University Press.

Williams, T.M. (ed.) (1986) *The impact of television: a national experiment in three communities*. New York: Academic Press.

Wilson, J.Q. and Kelling, G.W. (1982) 'Broken Windows' *Atlantic Monthly*, 249 (3), 29–38.

Wilson, P., Lincoln, R. and Koscis, R. (1997) 'Validity, utility and ethics of profiling for serial violent and sexual offences' *Psychiatry, Psychology and Law*, 4, 1–11.

Wilson, S. (1980) 'Vandalism and "defensible space" on London housing estates' in R.V.G. Clarke and P. Mayhew (eds) *Designing Out Crime*. London: HMSO.

Wulach, J. (1988) 'The criminal personality as a DSM-III-R antisocial, narcissistic, borderline and histrionic personality disorder' *International Journal of Offender Therapy and Comparative Criminology*, 32, 185–199.

Yochelson, S. and Samenow, S. (1976) *The Criminal Personality*. New York: Jason Aronson.

Yuille, J.C. and Cutshall, J.L. (1986) 'A case study of eyewitness memory of a crime' *Journal of Applied Psychology*, 71, 291–301.

Yule, W. and Brown, B.J. (1987) 'Some behavioural applications with juvenile offenders outside North America' in E.K. Morris and C.J. Braukmann (eds) *Behavioural approaches to crime and delinquency: a handbook of application, research and concepts*. New York: Plenum.

Zamble, E. (1990) 'Behavioural and psychological considerations in the success of prison reform' in J.W. Murphy and J.E. Dison (eds)

Are prisons any better? 20 years of prison reform. Newbury Park, CA: Sage.

Zamble, E. and Porporino, F.J. (1988) *Coping, behaviour and adaptation in prison inmates.* Berlin: Springer-Verlag.

Zimbardo, P.G. (1967) 'The psychology of police confessions' *Psychology Today*, 1, 17–27.

Index

THE HENLEY COLLEGE LIBRARY